Jose El Diablo
The World's Most Traveled Dog

Written By T. E. Quale & Bea Baker

Re-writes, Edited, & Production

by

Allen Kelly

ABOUT JOSE

During the nearly ten years that Jose lived, he traveled approximately four to five thousand miles by plane a month with his parents. A conservative figure would be over five hundred thousand miles by plane in his lifetime. He should be in the Guinness book of records as the most traveled dog by plane in the world.

PREFACE

This is a (mostly) true story of my life and travels with my human parents. If you have ever had a close relationship with a poodle or any other four legged friend you will understand the empathy that exists between the two.

Now I must tell you how it came about that I am telling this story instead of my mother or father. To begin with, I see this world and all that is in it from a different vantage point than they do. First of all, being the smallest and smartest member of the family gave me certain advantages of observation that were denied my parents.

Also, I was blessed with a wonderful sense of humor and great charm. If this sounds conceited, perhaps I am.

There is and always will be a very narrow line between the make believe world and the world of reality. Sometimes it is difficult know exactly when we cross over that line. So bear with me and enjoy my wanderings from the real world into that other realm of joyful escape from the mundane existence of daily living.

As you read and I hope enjoy my story, I am sure you will forgive both my fantasies and my vanity.

Jose El Diablo - The Worlds Most Traveled Dog

ISBN-13: 978-0692589106 (Custom)
ISBN-10: 0692589104

Copyright Allen Kelley and T.E. Quale. All rights reserved. Printed in the United States of America. No part of the publication may be reproduced, stored in a retrieval system or transmitted, in any form or by any means, electronic, mechanical, photocopying, recording or otherwise, without the prior written permission of the publisher.

For educational discounts – send email to the following email address. redrockwriters@gmail.com

Manufactured in the United States of America.
987654321

Doggie Quotes

Happiness is a warm puppy.
Charles M. Schulz

My little dog - a heartbeat at my feet.
Edith Wharton

They never talk about themselves but listen to you while you talk about yourself and keep up an appearance of being interested in the conversation.
Jerome K. Jerome

There's no psychiatrist in the world like a puppy licking your face.
Bernard Williams

Dogs are our link to paradise. They don't know evil or jealousy or discontent. To sit with a dog on a hillside on a glorious afternoon is to be back in Eden, where doing nothing was not boring - it was peace.
Milan Kundera

Dogs are miracles with paws.
Susan Ariel Rainbow Kennedy

My goal in life is to be as good of a person as my dog already thinks I am.
Author Unknown

My dog is usually pleased with what I do, because she's not infected with the concept of what I should be doing.
Lonzo Idolswine

To err is human -to forgive, canine.
Author Unknown

You think dogs will not be in heaven? I tell you, they will be there long before any of us.
Robert Louis Stevenson

Dogs are not our whole life, but they make our lives whole.
Roger Caras

If a dog will not come to you after having looked you in the face, you should go home and examine your conscience.
Woodrow Wilson

Whoever said you can't buy happiness forgot little puppies.
Gene Hill

In order to really enjoy a dog, one doesn't merely try to train him to be semi-human. The point of it is to open oneself to the possibility of becoming partly a dog.
Edward Hoagland

A dog is not 'almost human', and I know of no greater insult to the canine race than to describe it as such.
John Holmes

The greatest love is a mother's; then a dog's; then a sweetheart's.
Polish Proverb

No philosophers so thoroughly comprehend us as dogs and horses.
Herman Melville

There is no faith which has never yet been broken, except that of a truly faithful dog.
Konrad Lorenz

Children are for people who can't have dogs.
Author Unknown

If you can look at a dog and not feel vicarious excitement and affection, you must be a cat.
Author Unknown

The more one gets to know of men, the more one values dogs.
Alphonse Toussenel

Heaven goes by favor. If it went by merit, you would stay out and your dog would go in.
Mark Twain

If you are a dog and your owner suggests you wear a sweater....suggest he wear a tail.
Fran Lebowitz

You can say any fool thing to a dog, and the dog will give you this look that says, "My God, you're right! I never would've thought of that!"
Dave Barry

A dog is one of the few remaining reasons why some people can be persuaded to go for a walk.
Orlando A. Battista

Dog, n. A subsidiary Deity designed to catch the overflow and surplus of the world's worship . . . His master works for the means wherewith to purchase the idle wag of the Solomonic tail, seasoned with a look of tolerant recognition.
Ambrose Bierce

Dogs laugh, but they laugh with their tails.
Max Eastman

Scratch a dog and you'll find a permanent job.
Franklin P. Jones

Did you ever notice when you blow in a dog's face he gets mad at you? But when you take him in a car he sticks his head out the window?
Steve Bluestone

The most affectionate creature in the world is a wet dog.
Ambrose Bierce

Chapter One
I Knew A Good Thing

My human mother's diary, which I occasionally consulted for details when writing this mini-epic, didn't cover my conception, birth and the first few months of puppyhood, so I must rely on my memory and hearsay to tell you how I acquired my two adoring slaves. These "slaves" were actually my Mom and Dad from Palm Springs, California.

They had heard of my birth and were interested in buying a poodle of such of such excellent pedigree for their grandchildren. Fate had intervened.

The family that they intended me for, in some strange way had been persuaded to adopt a little mixed breed female, not at all in my class. If that family were capable of such an error in judgment, they were certainly not for me! Thank goodness my original owner (if I may use such a crude term, for nobody really owns a dog; either we own them, or are independent of then) immediately tried to persuade this interested couple to take me for themselves.

I was instantly pleased with them, even though they only had the capacity to love, they claimed there was just no way that they could take me. It was up to me to show them that it could be done. As I lay in my puppy basket, next to my poodle mother, I realized the enormity of my task. They traveled some five days a week on business, usually by plane. How on earth could they fit me into their lives? I was a little unsure myself, but soon discovered many ways.

The first step was accomplished; they actually took me with them to Palm Springs. We arrived on a Friday night. I did everything I could think of to make them love me! That first night they placed me in a large box filled with a pillow and blanket. The box was pulled close to the bedside, and the women (she was not yet 'Mom') hung one hand over the edge of the bed so that she could comfort me. I actually, comforted her. I nibbled and licked her hand until we both fell asleep. I was only three months old and as dear a dog as you have ever seen. The 'fitting' was beginning well.

The next morning it was The easy to see we were all molding like a hand in a glove. Their conversation had already changed to the right direction-me! After breakfast we went shopping. They bought a basket and a pillow to my liking. Kibble and milk bones were purchased. All these made me a little more confident and I worked even harder at being charming.

The man, who had some unfortunate reservations about dainty little poodles, then saw a plaid case. It looked much like a regular piece of luggage - except for an opening which allowed air in. I wasn't sure of its purpose but the man and woman's conversation revealed that it was designed for travelling. They bought it, confirming that I already so "fit in"! I was to accompany them on their journeys. I relaxed. They no longer had the mere capacity to love. They did love me.

Now it was safe to name me. This was the main subject of their conversation that Saturday. "Jose El Diablo" was decided upon. I was partly responsible for the unusual name; their choice of dinner the night before was responsible for the rest. They had eaten Mexican food on Friday night and the bites they offered me were swallowed eagerly. "Did we get a French poodle or a Mexican poodle?" they asked each other. My very large, dark brown eyes, set off by my light blond hair (my pedigree listed me as an apricot poodle) demanded something unique and unusual in names. "Jose El-Diablo" was the result. I assure you that I did not have an ounce of deviltry in my nature, which was as handsome as I.

Over that first weekend, they opened the travel kennel and allowed me to nap in it during the day. I found it very comfortable. By Monday morning, when it was time for them to return to a human thing called work, we were getting along just fine.

Our first trip was to be to Phoenix, Tucson, Denver, then back to Palm Springs. All went well from Palm Springs to Phoenix. I was not turned over to the attendant until just before the flight was scheduled for take-off. The attendant placed me in an air-conditioned compartment, which was comfortable. But I was lonely for I found out that I was so 'fit in' with these increasingly dear people I missed them. When they picked me up I made a terrible fuss over them. They were delighted with how pleased I was to see them. At this time, I should say that never once had I acted towards them. I had always truly liked them. But I realized then how much I loved them -- like parents. They were Mom and Dad from then on.

We drove to Tucson in a rental car. Mom and Dad worked there all day and then drove back to Phoenix. Again I was placed in the kennel and then in the little compartment. The flight was longer than the first, and when we arrived in Denver, the airline people boo-booed. parents waited and waited in the special area where people picked up their pets. Their own luggage arrived and but their most precious piece of luggage still did not. Finally, my father went back to the carousel where their regular luggage had arrived and there I was, going round and round, crown over paws. I was scared to death. I had gone down the regular luggage belt, down the chute and onto the carousel.

Mom and Dad were so angry they insisted on seeing the agent. They verbally decked him, and I backed them up by shaking and crying. I should have won an Oscar. (But, in all honesty, I didn't have to act -- I was truly shaken.) My father insisted on a letter of apology, a refund on my fare... and threatened never to travel on that airline again. My goodness, how I had fit in!

Our stay in Denver was profitable for my parents and very pleasant for me. I had grass to run in, marvelous food and lots of love. I dreaded the return trip. so did my parents. As we waited at the airport my parents tried to convince themselves that all would go well, but I could tell by the conversation that they were very apprehensive, which increased my own fears. Imagine my relief when just prior to boarding, my mother took a stand. She put me into my travel case and told Dad she was going to carry me on board and place me between the seats. And she did. we were all nervous wrecks for the first 20 minutes.

After we were airborne, we relaxed a little. I did my part by being as quiet as a mouse. But just about the time we became smug over our success, we had a real fright. Because my case could just fit between the seats, Mom folded herself like an envelope. Her feet rested on top of my case. A young steward on the flight was most thoughtful and considerate -- too much so! When he noticed how cramped Mom was, he insisted moving my case to the luggage compartment for her comfort. And you should have heard her! She insisted that she was comfortable only when her knees were under her chin and her feet were the air.

Needless to say, I was shaking in my boots (well, if I had had boots I would have shaken in them!) Bless her heart-she won and that was the beginning of my illicit travels. My parents wasted no time purchasing a new case, which was about half the size of the first. It was a regular piece of luggage with a zipper on its top and side. Mom showed her ingenuity. She cut three air holes in the side, removed the lining and replaced it with an old fishnet stocking. This new case was not as spacious as the first, but I was willing to sacrifice some comfort to fit in with my parents. Over the weekend we practiced. Mom placed me in the case and we walked around the pool area and then rode in the car. I also used it as a place to nap--well, I was still a puppy! I know she was worried about my comfort, so I reassured her by climbing into it myself. I did everything but zip the case.

When it was again time to resume our travels, procedures differed. Dad checked in and went immediately to the gate. Mom kept me in the lady's room until ten minutes before boarding. I did my part by being ready and willing to hop into my case. However, complete discretion was impossible. Being such a handsome young fellow with my apricot hair and lovely eyes, I was never inconspicuous. Everyone stopped to either talk to me or about me, so there were times on our travels when it was difficult for Mom to slip me into my case unnoticed.

All went well on that trip and subsequent trips. Two or three weeks passed without close calls. Once in or around an airport or a plane I never made a sound. But when at home I could bark and run as much as I wished. And I did a lot of it to make up for my noiselessness. And, being beautiful, I had an equally wonderful voice.

I was also well-behaved at the hotels. I soon found out that the finer they were, the more

Chapter One I Knew A Good Thing

welcomed they made me feel.

And many times, when the help could not recall my parents' names, they could recall mine. Mom and Dad always laughed about that, which proves how wonderful they were--no wonder we always got along!

But I had a home life too. I had received my first baby shots in Fresno, which was my first home. (Yes! I'll admit it! I was not always the Palm Springs sophisticate!) Once settled in with Mom and Dad, it came time to have my first adult shots. I felt I was a little young-- only four months-but the veterinarian assured Mom that I needed four shots at two week intervals. The purpose, so I understood, was to make me immune to "all sorts of things." I also received a rabies shot which the doctor laughingly told Mom that I was now licensed to bite. I was a bit disappointed when mom gave the doctor the satisfaction of laughing at his tasteless joke. The first and second adult shots were a breeze. To be absolutely honest, I didn't even feel the needle. But I got my Moms sympathy by whining a bit. The third shot... that was another affair.

When we arrived at the vet, the nurse casually mentioned that Dr. Jackson had a new assistant, a Dr. Baker. The silly fact that my parents and this vet shared a surname convinced the nurse that he would be great for us. It was beyond my apricot-colored head how humans think as they do. We entered the usual room and I was placed on the cold table, which I was becoming used to.

A pleasant young man came in and introduced himself as Dr. Baker. Before my mother could open her mouth to say "Hello," or "Get the hell out of here," he picked up a prepared needle, picked me up with his other hand and joined us together without a single thought to my comfort. I shrieked! The good Dr. Jackson would have eased it in, but that clod-who should have been shooting up horses, not dainty little dogs--punctured me like a balloon. My mother was so angry she chewed the nurse out, saying she drove miles further than necessary because she wanted Dr. Jackson. The nurse apologized, and wrote on my card "Dr. Jackson only." To be honest--and dogs are creatures with great integrity - I had, by then, recovered from the pain. But when I saw how upset my poor mother was, I just hated to let the opportunity for some extra sympathy and attention pass by. So, on the way home, every time Mom as much as touched me, I let out the most pitiful cry ever emitted by any four legged species. By the time we reached home, my poor Mom was sickest at heart and had to go to bed.

She and Dad carried me in my basket to the kitchen where I could watch them. each time they touched me, I manufactured agony. Now, I did not intend to go as far as I did, but all the special attention was fun. I eventually paid for it because Mom called Dr. Jackson and told him what pain I had been in since receiving the shot. He assured Mom that it was not normal (he was so right!) and that she should bring me back. 0 no!

I started to cry. I knew I would be found out. They carried me to the car, down the road and back into Dr. Jackson's office, lapped in a pillow like the invalid I was not.

I continued to moan, cry and carry on. But when Dr. Jackson took me in hand I was so frightened and embarrassed, I shut up. You should have seen Mom's face. I am sure the doctor thought she one of those neurotic women whose world rotates on their little dog's axis. He tried to comfort her by saying "Haven't you ever gone to the dentist with a toothache to have it stop while in the lobby?" He gave me another shot of something that looked like water and probably was a placebo. My mother took me to the car where

Chapter One I Knew A Good Thing

my father anxiously waited, not being able to stand my misery. Dear man I tried to emote dreadful pain, but they were too angry and embarrassed to offer any sympathy. I did learn a lesson about integrity, however. It's the best policy.

After this we sere soon on our way to Salt Lake with a change of planes in Las Vegas. Perhaps it was the shot, or perhaps something I had eaten - I had an awful stomach ache. I was struck with cramps shortly after the plane ascended. I knew Mom and Dad were in agony for me and for themselves. Mom tried to discreetly rub my tummy but nothing helped. Everybody around us knew that I was in the bag-poodle contraband! Fortunately, we had 45 minutes between planes, so I was taken for a walk outside the terminal. My stomach ache vanished upon relieving myself. You see--I was sincerely capable of pain.

Chapter Two
Further Travels and the Doctor

My parents wasted no time purchasing a new case, which was about half the size of the first. It was a regular piece of luggage with a zipper on its top and side. Mom showed her ingenuity. She cut three air holes in the side, removed the lining and replaced it with an old fishnet stocking.

This new case was not as spacious as the first, but I was willing to sacrifice some comfort to fit in with my parents. Over the weekend we practiced. Mom placed me in the case and we walked around the pool area and then rode in the car. I also used it as a place to nap--well, I was still a puppy! I know she was worried about my comfort, so I reassured her by climbing into it myself. I did everything but zip the case.

When it was again time to resume our travels, procedures differed. Dad checked in and went immediately to the gate. Mom kept me in the lady's room until ten minutes before boarding. I did my part by being ready and willing to hop into my case. However, complete discretion was impossible. Being

Chapter Two Further Travels and the Doctor

such a handsome young fellow with my apricot hair and lovely eyes, I was never inconspicuous. Everyone stopped to either talk to me or about me, so there were times on our travels when it was difficult for Mom to slip me into my case unnoticed.

All went well on that trip and consequent trips. Two or three weeks passed without close calls. Once in or around an airport or a plane I never made a sound. But when at home I could bark and run as much as I wished. And I did a lot of it to make up for my noiselessness on planes. And, being beautiful, I had an equally wonderful voice.

I was also well-behaved at the hotels. I soon found out that the finer they were, the more welcomed they made me feel.

Chapter Three
Pet Therapy

I grew into a handsome dog and traveled by plane so much that it became quite routine. My apricot curls and I had been seen at all the best hotels in the west: the St. Francis in San Francisco; the Utah in Salt Lake City; the Century Plaza in Beverly Hills; the Benson and the Sheraton Hotels in Seattle. I was welcomed and fussed over nearly everywhere we went. But my parents refused to be wishy-washy sops who allowed their pampered to tromp all over them. They made a number of rules to be kept once I began traveling with them: I must never be allowed on the furniture. Never on allowed on the bed. Never to be fed at the table. For stalwart types, they gave in very quickly; all the rules were cast to the wind within one week.

Dad was coming along quite well. At first he was extremely self-conscious when he took me on my early morning walk. But he was soon made comfortable at each hotel when he found several owners or bellboys taking dogs on their constitutional up and down and around the block. I was the handsomest, of course, --no pride, just integrity! I tried to show off my equally agreeable personality by learning quickly about good manners.

Because of my presence, they were having new and interesting experiences. One day, Mom walked me in a small park at Lloyd Center just across the street from the Portland Sheraton Hotel. A woman with a black standard poodle stopped to admire me. And, my mother complimented the lady's friend. His name was Jock. Their conversation soon revealed that both Mom and this lady--whose name was Ellsworth--both enjoyed talking to their pets. But I soon found out that Jock was a source of strength for Mrs. Ellsworth, rather than simple pleasure. She had suffered a very serious stroke which left her unable to speak. After several weeks she could make sounds and with concentration, could form words. But this advance was also frustrating for the words would not come out the way she had formed them in her mind. To get out a short sentence would take agonizing seconds. This naturally embarrassed her and she refused to converse with people. Her doctor told her that only practice would bring back her speech and that she gets a pet and talk to it. Jock was her choice.

We dogs are far finer (and much more intelligent) than our masters in many ways; most notably, we don't have nervous speech problems. We listen no matter what is said, or how said. Within six months Mrs. Ellsworth improved so much she could talk easily with people. As a matter of fact, one could not detect a thing wrong with her speech. Isn't it amazing what we dogs are capable of doing!

While my mother and Mrs. Ellsworth talked, we walked until we came upon a sandy place with a bench in a shaded area. We sat down and they released Jock and me.

We investigated every bush and tree in the

area, adn1ired each other and gossiped a bit. After a half-hour, a very pleasant gentlemen arrived who was no stranger to Jock and his mother.

Mrs. Ellsworth introduced her husband as executive chef of the Sheraton Hotel. Get the idea? He told Mom that any time she would like some very meaty prime ribs (which are my favorite) she could just call and receive all I could manage to eat. I could understand why Jock was so well nourished. Ellsworth stressed that the ribs would not be scrappy remains. My mouth watered. That very evening we took advantage of his kindness; meaning I had a delicious dinner.

Our travels took us next to Las Vegas. This desert city did not require my parents to stop there often during the year. After my parents had discovered how welcome I was at this fine hotel, they put all caution aside and carried me into the lobby of the Desert Inn with all the pride they could muster.

We swiftly learned that we should not have laid aside all caution. Of all the places in the world that would object to a pet! Crazy, gambling, immoral Las Vegas. They had half-naked dancers in their shows, but objected to a well-furred poodle! "You wouldn't even look up if someone walked in with a snake around their neck," my mother protested. They resisted her objections and declared "we have made wonderful arrangements for them to be picked up and kenneled, just across the street." I began to shake. Mom did her usual fast thinking- I think that woman had incredible instinct! "Oh," she replied, "he doesn't belong to me. He's my sister's, who will not be staying here." Then she casually went to the car, placed me in my bag, and nonchalantly walked by the front desk.

A very un-casual tip to the maid secured my comfort and stay at the Desert Inn. Fortunately, our room was in a location where Dad could take me out undetected by a stairway.

Chapter Three Pet Therapy

I was in a huff about my treatment until we found out that the barring of pets was based on sound reason. In Las Vegas, people would forget their pets once they entered the casinos. Humanitarianism formed part of the reason, the other was profit. People staying in the hotel would be disturbed by the unhappy sounds of a lonesome animal. My parents later found a smaller hotel that made me welcome whenever it was necessary for my parents to spend time in Las Vegas.

You will have noticed how well I cooperated with my parents. I was genial about the traveling bag, even though I was not happy when confined to it. But I had learned to love my parents as much as they loved me. If I were uncomfortable at times, I knew that the only way that they could "improve" the situation would be to leave me at home or at a kennel.

I sometimes found out that there was a fly in the ointment — or in the dog food. We were in Los Angeles enjoying our stay at the Sheraton West Hotel. Across the street was a lovely little park, a marvelous place to run. One evening my and Mom and Dad took me there to get some exercise. They removed leash and I ran like the wind. It was so windy I grew careless about a flight of steps. I had been up and down them several times, but that night, I let my caution float with the wind. With my parents behind me, I started down those treacherous steps. For some reason I excitedly turned to see if they were still behind me.

I don't exactly know what happened, but I promptly tumbled to the bottom. When I tried to get up, my pride was bruised. I found my right hind leg unable to support me. My hip or knee was thrown out of joint. I was in terrible pain — real pain, not that silly stuff dreamed up for attention.

My mother was doing everything she could to sooth the pain, which, ironically caused more pain. She finally realized that my leg was hurt and holding me only worsened it.

With Dad's help, she straightened it —Ye God! What a noise that made! She gently rubbed it until the pain eased and the joint rotated into place. I was finally able to stand on it and even run a little. I found comfort in knowing how relieved my folks were. That I was apparently well. But, sad to say: I was not unscathed. The next day the leg kept slipping from its place. I hobbled about on three legs, resembling an apricot-colored Captain Ahab.

This went on for two weeks. I was in pain more than I deserved to be. Dr. Jackson was the man to see. He tested the muscles of my injured leg with his usual gentle thoroughness and told my anxious mother that the muscles were so badly damaged that I needed-an operation. Even though I did not know at the time what an operation meant, I could tell by his serious demeanor that it was not some new kind of dog treat! Quite the opposite! He told her that that I should have my operation' soon, as the younger I was, the better. We went home, my parents discussing the situation and deciding to have the surgery done the following Friday. This would give me a long weekend to recuperate. We were not due in the air until Tuesday! The week between I tried my best to walk on my injured, leg even though it gave me a lot of pain. I hoped to avoid the operation, whatever it was.

Somedays, I almost succeeded. Other days though, I would have to hop along on three legs.

I wasn't alone in my rationalizations. On the way to the hospital that Friday, Mom and Dad talked all the way of how much better I seemed to be. Perhaps the doctor would think an operation was unnecessary.

No such luck. As soon as were in the doctor's office my folks eagerly mentioned how much better I was walking. Dr. Jackson called for a demonstration. I did my best not to limp, but my wretched leg betrayed me. The doctor pointed out that the knee was slipping out of joint and explained that the injury would always give me trouble if not repaired. The 'operation' was on.

The doctor gave me a shot of something. I became drowsy while wondering if I was going to sleep through the operation, when I was able to hear my parents asking when I could come home. Dr. Jackson wanted to keep me for a couple of days, but Mom and Dad didn't want to leave me. They claimed that I would be scared to stay at the veterinarian's office (well, maybe they were a little bit right about that). They won out. That didn't make me too happy! (Thanks for your tenacity Mom and Dad.)

Then, everything became faraway to me. I could hear Dr. Jackson tell them he would call when they could pick me up.

I plummeted into sleep, knowing I would not be left alone in some place where no one would pay attention to my cries — and I intended to do some crying. A smart dog never lets opportunities for extra attention slip by.

Upon awakening I found out that an operation was more than enforced sleep. Whatever had happened to me was far worse than I had anticipated. I had gone under at about 8:00 and it was 2:00 when I finally grew conscious of a very painful knee. An equally hurtful headache kept it company. I heard pitiful moans and they were coming from me.

Soon, a nurse entered. She patted me, murmured some comforting words and told the doctor that I was awake. He came in, took a look at me, fondled my head and called me 'a good little fellow.' I already knew that, but it was nice to hear it. The nurse called my folks and told them they could fetch me. I would have liked to lick her hand in appreciation, but I was way too miserable to do this. I wondered if some supernatural doggy tribunal was punishing me for the pain I pretended to have some months earlier.

About a half-hour later, my parents' voices were heard. I had been keeping my cries to small, sad moans, but now I screamed and cried in ripping, heartbreaking tones that only a lonesome, hurt dog can produce. My poor parents were almost in tears when they saw my head shaved down to the flesh and decorated with stiches. Dr. Jackson explained that I would bite off any covering and the air would prove its best healer. Home we went, my groggy body resting on the pillow. Each time I tried to move the pain was excruciating and my cries cleaved my parents' hearts in two.

Back home, they saw to my comfort. I was placed in my basket with a light blanket over me. Dad put my basket on the kitchen table so that I could watch my mother without raising my head, my eyes following her. We had only been home for a few minutes when our neighbor, Dooley, came in to inquire about me. Dooley was a great joker. When I first met him I wasn't sure I was going to like him. We poodles can be notorious for our lack of humor, but I wasn't an ordinary poodle so I decided I would try.

Soon I found out that he was a fine fellow. His wife, Bobby, loved me too. The reason I was unsure about Dooley at the beginning was something he said to my father when I was very young. We male dogs lack a good sense of balance when we are young and so must squat like females for several months. Mom and Dad were having a drink-they needed one after what I had put them through! They poured one for Dooley and then all three hashed over my operation. Dooley leaned over to look at my incision when mom plucked back my cover. As he moved in for a good look, I screamed the way only a dog can scream.

Dooley practically dropped his drink and made for the door as if demons were after him. It took both Mom and Dad to calm him. Shakily, he finished his drink. But they were chuckling, and so was I. My pain vanished for a moment.

Later that evening, realizing to what noble heights I had raised my parents: they were planning to take sacrificial holding and comforting me all night. I decided to show them that I was equally noble. (I had to return some of the love and kindness they showered on me!)

When it came time to retire, they placed my basket next to them. I had never used the basket except for naps in the early days. My regular place was now, of course, anywhere that I was comfortable-usually the bed. It was my bad leg; I was perfectly willing to spend the night in my abandoned basket. Mom was afraid I would miss being in the bed, so she gently placed me next to her. I realized that if I stayed there she would not sleep (and with the afternoon I had put her through, she needed it!) so I moaned and put my apricot head over the side of the bed, indicating my wish to stay in my basket. Of course, they understood. They placed me in my basket, tucked me in and settled into what they were sure would be a sleepless night. I managed to fool them; I remained quiet. Every time I tried to turn over, I was in great pain, but I stifled my moans. There's a time to cry and a time not to cry.

The next morning, they were well rested and made a deservedly fuss over me.

The trip back to the hospital was brief and not unpleasant. The doctor was pleased with my progress and gave my mother permission to take me to Los Angeles. He also gave her permission to bring me back immediately if my incision swelled.

We drove to Los Angeles Tuesday morning

and stayed at the Sheraton Hotel. I was always welcomed there and there was a nice grassy spot where I could run and sniff the canine grapevine. Out-of-town chatter and gossip was always nice to hear. The following Friday when I had my stitches removed, I didn't feel a thing. Dr. Jackson declared me healed and discharged me. Only time was needed to conceal the scar. I was very self-conscious of that bare spot because people would constantly ask Mom how I had injured myself. Some even though Mom and Dad had been careless enough to allow me to be hit by a car! Honestly!

Shortly after my operation, we travelled to Fresno. Ah-can you go home again? In my case, yes. We visited the home where my poodle mother and father lived. They were surprised to see how their puppy had grown, and it was gratifying for me to see them again. My poodle mother was impressed with my sophistication and independence, for I covered more miles in one week than she had or would in her life. Nonetheless, she scolded me like I was a child who had never been away from home. I good naturedly humored her and even pretended to cry when she was cross with me) well, maybe I didn't entirely pretend!). My folks were very amused at us. I found myself hoping we would go back often, for the ties were very strong. I was thinking upon this when she told me, in our private language that she would always be with me. "You may live with humans, but you are a dog. No more, but no less. You will see me at the last." I didn't know what she meant by this, but I took comfort, even though I was not in pain.

Chapter Four
The Ho! Ho Season and Snow Fall Turned To Winter

Palm Springs is famous for its lack of snow, so it was in Denver and Salt Lake that I first encountered this wonderful soft, white stuff.

In anticipation of winter travelling, Mom designed and knit an ingenious navy blue sweater for me. It covered my long legs, fit snugly about my body and buttoned down the back. However, it did not impede me from seeing to the necessary comforts. Overlaid with a red wool coat, I was able to attract the rightful amount of attention. Frankly, I was downright glamorous, with my white fur frothing against the bright red — blue clothing, making me look like a patriotic snow prince. White, did you ask? I thought you were apricot! My original coat color had turned a startling, beautiful white.

In Salt Lake City, we stayed at the Utah Hotel. Dad took me down for my morning romp, dressed in my tres-chic winter wear. I was admiring myself until my attention was distracted by the sight of fluffy white stuff blanketing the ground. It looked like feathers, but when I stuck my paw into it, I found it cold and damp. I tried to roll in it, but the white stuff stuck to my wool coat and began to melt.

Coinciding with my maturity was a wonderful time of year that you could feel in the air, whether in the snow or in desert. People spoke of it: Christmas, parties, love, hope. It sounded wonderful. Everywhere we went, the streets were brightly trimmed. We bought items which Mom would conceal from sight with paper and bright ribbons. Christmas was mysterious, but enjoyable in its drama.

About a week before the actual day of Christmas we drove into Los Angeles. We stopped several times and delivered gaily wrapped packages. Finally arriving at the Century Plaza Hotel, we took all the remaining gifts to our suite. Mom and Dad piled all the packages on top of the table in a very festive display. They hurried to the hotel store and bought soft drinks, cheese, chips and liquor. I looked on and wondered, and delighted.

Mom and Dad had just returned to our room when there was an ominous knock on the door. Could this be a signal as to the wonderful events of the evening that were forthcoming?

We then marched to a different room in great anticipation. The door to this room opened to reveal a most fascinating clan including a four legged family member (Mimi). We were greeted by Sally and Jerry Rasevear and their 3 children. After enthusiastic greetings, we all plunged into the goodies and drinks. I took water with tidbits and frisked around a lot.

After the first round of drinks, Dad started in the pile of gifts, passing out one at a time so that everybody could enjoy the person receiving a gift opening his or her package. I received a couple of presents too-from Mimi, whom I was very disappointed not to see at the party. Mimi, of course, was another dog. Frankly, she was ugly, but I loved her anyway, for she had made me realize and understand. the nature of my gender. In other words, the fact that she was female and I was male, meant something! That was a memorable decision but I assure you, nothing happened! We were nine months old at the time and she was at the tail of something called 'in heat.' I overheard somebody say that Mimi was in 'no danger.' I figured out that the 'no danger' referred to me in a roundabout way. Ah, but she was danger! It was love at first sniff. I tried with some lovemaking, but somebody always interfered. Eventually we were segregated, with me in the house and her out of the house, and vice versa. Sally remarked "Maybe next time," because Mimi was 'too young.' That was a matter of opinion! instincts told me I was old enough. Mimi's special perfume also assured me that there was no problem with her age.

Well, enough of that questionable subject! The children were delighted with their gifts and so were the adults. Packages opened, their contents removed, the room tidied up, and all went to the Granada Room for dinner. Everyone but me, but that was fine. I was exhausted with excitement. I barked a bit in show, but when the door closed, I wholeheartedly claimed the bed.

Several hours later, they returned. Mom was carrying my favorite snack in a bag; the wonderful aroma of prime rib could not be mistaken. While everybody busied themselves bundling me up for a walk, Mom called the desk and requested another bed be placed in our room. I wished to protest that I did not need a bed-the king-sized one was fine, even with Mom and Dad in it. But it was not meant for me-the three grandchildren were going to stay the night. At first I didn't feel particularly usurped, for the three children were good-natured and a lot of fun. The children wanted to stay and there was added convenience of Sally, their mother having a dental appointment about ten blocks from the hotel in the morning.

After the parents left, we got ready for bed and then began the process of fitting six people into two beds. Suzy shared the king with Mom and Dad, which meant that I had been usurped after all. Two of the children slept in the double. I wandered all over the place that night, first nudging one body and then another. Where did I sleep? I don't remember now.

We had breakfast in the room and then dashed out to deliver other gifts and make purchases. We were back in time for Jerry to pick up the children. We parted with many wishes for Happy Holidays and Merry Christmas. That evening we drove back to Palm Springs.

Home Christmas rituals followed. I watched while Dad strung lights around the house and Mom trimmed the living room and Christmas tree. I puzzled over the human that brought a tree into the house, but forgot my puzzlement in admiration, for it was very lovely when Mom finished decorating it with ornaments. My admiration caused me to play with a few of the ornaments. After breaking one and suffering a scolding, I admired without touching from then on.

I understood that this Christmas was to be different from the ones they usually had. This idea delighted me in a round about way, for I realized that this Christmas came once every year. Every year we could have a tree in the house, parties with friends and families, and lots of festivity and cheer. This year, rather than Mom and Dad traveling to Los Angeles to spend Christmas Eve with one family and then Christmas Day with the other family, our oldest family would be dropping by our Palm Springs house on December 27th on their way home from the Utah snow country.

So, after a Christmassy whirl of parties, the Eve found just the three of us at home together. My parents had drinks and homemade tamales in front of the fireplace. I, at first, missed the bustle of people but soon learned the charm of a quiet Christmas Eve. I also learned that this glittery, merry human holiday was more than a tree, gifts, cocktails, and colored lights. There had been a birth of great importance connected with the holiday, one that meant hope and joy to many people. I didn't know who was born-just that it was someone called 'Christ' born a long time ago, yet born again every year on the same day. I pondered this while wondering about presents from my parents. There was a package that contained a chewy shoe and a new rawhide bone. Christmas Eve was spent reducing the bone to pulp.

Even after Christmas there was still a huge pile of gifts left over. Our oldest and largest family arrived on the 27th to claim them. But first they all took a swim in our pool which was kept at 88 degrees. They then had goodies and drinks and left for dinner. I was so tired that I preferred to stay home. That's not quite the Truth-I wanted to go that time, but there was some stupid law against dogs entering restaurants and markets. I didn't understand it, because I saw big two-legged types with hair down to their shoulders freely entering the same places.

At least, I was always neat and washed, and poodles don't shed. It was a case of discrimination, or stupidity on somebody's part. But if that's all I had to complain about, I should remain quiet. Besides, with all the joy of Christmas, bitterness was out of place.

Napping while they were gone, I was rested

for their home coming, but not for the festivities which happened afterwards. Everybody made short work of the intriguing pile. I was glad to accept several little stuffed animals. I also found it great sport to nip off their eyes, bite off their ears as well as dismembering other parts.

There was lots of kissing and thanking going on. I liked and made happy sounds, and grew happier remembering that this time would come again next year. And the next, and the next ...

At that time, it did not occur to me that eventually my years would come to an end-no more Christmas for me. I remembered my poodle mother's words and worries what they meant. But I did not worry enough to be sad. I had many years and much joy to experience ahead of me.

Chapter Five
New York and a New Adventure

The big family left the next day. We all took our time getting up, getting into the pool and eating breakfast alfresco. Soon it was time for them to leave. Mom was disappointed because they could not spend more time with us, but it was fine with me. I know that sounds mean, but a houseful of people was wearing on my nerves, as well as depriving me of my deserved attention. I loved them all, but I was very happy to spend a quiet normal dinner in front of the television set. We were in bed early.

The following week was fairly quiet. I didn't realize that everybody was coiling for another outbreak of merriment on the last day of the year. The folks played golf. I rode on the cart with them. Nobody ever objected, because I looked so elegant sitting there with those handsome people. I never could understand why Mom and Dad and so many other people liked to knock a little white ball around, but they probably wondered why I liked to roll and

Chapter Five   New York and a New Adventure

romp on the tight, velvety grass and then investigate the trees, a paradise of smelly-gossip.

There was a party for Mom's sisters and their husbands. Saturday was a slow day of routine and riding about in the golf cart. And then came Sunday, which was New Year's Eve. This was another human celebration, a lot more secular than Christmas. Another party, this time with friends. Once more, I had lots of attention and goodies, but wondered what the excitement was all about. This celebration was far different from Christmas, although something new was about to be born.

The new thing was a new year.

At midnight, the time of the birth, Dad uncorked the champagne and everyone toasted. I really couldn't tell the old year from the new one, but I celebrated too. The party didn't break up until 3:30 A.M. We didn't crawl out of bed until 9:00 and then hurried around to breakfast in front of the television to watch the Rose Parade. Television gives me a headache, but I watched carefully, for the floats were very lovely.

Golf consumed the afternoon of the first day of the new year. I stayed in the cart, too tired to frisk, and depressed about the following day for Mom had made an appointment for me to be groomed. I was sorry now that I had been such a smart aleck about my body, not allowing her gentle hands to trim inside my ears and around my toes. But I was a ticklish creature. We turned in at 9:00. Holidays are great but tiring. I was the first to fall asleep, eschewing the nightly ritual of romping on the bed with Dad.

Mom and Dad always swam before breakfast. When at home, I would caper about the pool, running from end to end and licking their faces when they popped out of the water. I didn't like the chlorine, but they got a tremendous kick out of it and it was something I could do to show them how happy I was. Human beings needed to know this.

The swim was regrettably short and breakfast rushed, as we had an early appointment at that miserable parlor. The clippers promised to have me ready by noon.

The bath came first. I thought it unnecessary because Mom bathed me twice a week with something called Vita-Bathe. It must have been terribly expensive because when she told people she dunked her poodle in it, they gasped and remarked about not being able to afford it for themselves.

I was lathered up, rinsed and dried. The insides of my ears were worked on. The two attractive young ladies who operated the parlor made us as pretty as possible. The ladies were punctual and had me ready at 11:45. Mom arrived about 20 minutes later. I had admired myself several times in the mirror and was not at all surprised that several other pets of the opposite gender were admiring me too. Of course I had long been aware of this simple yet vital difference between the sexes, and was now growing aware of strange, perverse habits of lady dogs. They would roll their eyes and wag their tails as a come on. And when a fellow tried to come on-politely of course-they would nip and growl. But I certainly was not, in those days, ready to give-up the youthful, virile dog that I was. I felt that someday I would meet a dog that would signal and then yield to my affectionate nature.

Mom was delighted with my appearance and Dad just as pleased. My hair had been left long as added protection for the cold we were expecting to encounter in New York, our destination. But this shagginess only added to my charms. I realized that for all the trouble, the Poodle Parlor was worth it.

As I indicated, we were on our way to New York. Most of our trips were accomplished with a minimum of effort, but the flight to New York would be twice as long and my clothing, as already mentioned, needed special consideration. The packing finished, the house was locked, and we flew to Los Angeles to stay overnight at the International Hotel, situated next to LAX. Our plane was to leave at 9:00 A.M. the next morning and we wanted to make sure we caught our flight.

Our logic proved beneficial, for the airport was a madhouse. Bad eastern weather had stranded hundreds of people at the airport. Flight traffic was bad enough at his time every year with the Rose Bowl participants and other holiday travelers struggling homeward; bad weather aggravated the situation tenfold.

Fortunately, all was confirmed and we felt ourselves fortunate as we made our way through a lobby packed with people sleeping in chairs, on the floor, standing four-abreast at several restaurants. The folks wisely decided to eat in their room, and we were pleased not to be left alone for I did not like that hotel.

We all went to bed. I was up soon, wandering about, beset with my unexplainable dislike. I finally found what I didn't like about that hotel: the windows were sealed shut to screen the terrific noise. My parents slept well, but I paced the floor, jumped on chairs to look out the window, then paced some more. I tried in every way to pass the sleepless night without disturbing Mom and Dad, and I succeeded. But I didn't have an hour's sleep.

When the alarm sounded at 6:00 A.M. I was very groggy too much so to be my usual good-natured self. I improvised my sweet demeanor; in truth, I felt very blah, which made me angry.

I didn't know that Mom had secured some tranquilizers from Dr. Jackson. Just before we left for the airport, she drugged me. I was indignant over their treatment of me, for Dad held me while she stuffed one down my throat. I managed to spit it out twice before they rammed it down so far I had to keep it. Down it went. And up I went.

The pill should have made me sleepy but it accomplished the opposite – it made me a nervous wreck. The sleepless night contributed to my condition. When we were settled in the plane, I was overcome with the most horrible sensation of entrapment. Suddenly, I could not bear that travelling case. There had been times in the past when I had not been comfortable, but I had stayed patient and quiet. But that stupid pill rocketed me right out of my heretofore quiet head. I whimpered and clawed at the inside of my case. When Mom put her hand in to comfort me, I bit her. Hard!

She was as shocked as I was! I cringed in my case until I heard my parents talking to each other. There was
no hatred in their voices, only concern. I seized control of myself and finally dozed off.

A movie was shown on the flight which probably saved my curly white hide. The flight attendants did not move about the cabin which kept them from hearing my whimpers and moans. That four-hour flight seemed like a year.

As we finally began the approach to Kennedy Airport, I took a hard grip on myself. We left the plane undetected. I didn't want to look at Mom and Dad when we were safely landed, for I was sure I had taken away all the years I had given them. Though I did look hard at Mom when she declared I had given her new gray hairs.

Once out of the airport and out of the bag I started to feel better. It was about an hour's drive to New York City, in a big, comfortable cab with a quiet driver. I tried to stay alert but I was so exhausted, I couldn't stay awake.

The hotel welcomed me as I should be welcomed. Though they had never met me, and had not anticipated me, they reacted perfectly

Chapter Five New York and a New Adventure

by creating a big fuss over me.

We had a nice suite on the ninth floor. I looked the place over, tried the beds, and jumped one to the other several times before they realized I wanted them pushed together. After all, I was accustomed to a king-sized bed, and with the twin beds pushed together, I had room to stretch out.

After we were unpacked, we found a small all-night market. We purchased breakfast-stuff and a variety of goodies for me. After arranging to have it sent to the hotel, we walked back. Mom dressed me as warmly as she could in all my winter finery, previously displayed on the streets of Salt Lake City. I was still so cold I could barely walk. Dad finally picked me up and snuggled me in his coat. He then instructed Mom to buy me some boots the next day. He told her my paws were like ice. He did not exaggerate.

Even though we were in a strange hotel, Mom made me feel at home with some liverwurst, and later, some pet cookies and milk bone. She was so sweet to me. The next morning, Dad took his shower and Mom went in to dry his back. She was sweet to him, too. She then realized that it was snowing. He put on a robe and carried me to a window. Daylight was breaking. Large, beautiful, feathery pinwheels were drifting from the sky. It had been snowing all night, and there was not a single ugly thing about new-found beauty.

I was beginning to get uncomfortable in the way all mammals get uncomfortable. I needed to relieve myself, but was not eager to brave the cold. Dad bundled himself up while Mom bundled me. We descended. I rushed to the first of the several planter boxes in front of the hotel, relieved myself as quickly as I could, eschewed the usual sniff for doggy grapevine, and the usual wait for Dad to pick me up. I leaped into his arms and we retreated. I shook for about five minutes after we returned to our warm suite. I can't understand why anyone would want to live in such a cold place. Palm Springs was a heaven to this El Diablo!

Dad left for the office after breakfast. I felt sorry for him having to go out into the cold again. I learned that morning that I could expect two trips a year to New York, at the times the "buyers" were seeing all the 'new lines.' Dad liked to work with his people at the beginning of each new season.

Mom tidied our suite, bathed, dressed and then readied me. I was so cold I could only walk for a short distance. Mom ended up ferrying me inside her coat to the store. We made several purchases. One was a fur Cossack hat for Dad with flaps that could be pulled over his ears. She also bought him a gray wool scarf. For me, she bought two sweaters, and then two sets of boots. The only color available was red, but I was glad to have boots small enough for my petite feet. The boots had ribbon laced through two holes at the back, necessitating the need for four bows to be tied to secure the contrivances to my feet. Mom recognized how inefficient and time-wasting all that tying would be so her genius told her to buy a roll of transparent surgical tape. She then taped my boots onto me before we left the store. I took a few minutes to get used to them. It felt strange to have something attached to my feet; after all, I'm a California dog, the state which invented bare feet. But now I was able to walk without my paws turning ice cubes. We then bought some navy blue yarn, with which Mom knitted a new sweater for me. A few days later it was ready and I liked it better than my red one. It had a nice high turtleneck and looked smart with my blue all-weather coat. I was now also able to alternate outfits, increasing my reputation as a clothes dog. The bellboys claimed I was the best dressed pet in the hotel, if not in New York. When we walked through the stores or down the

Chapter Five New York and a New Adventure

streets, nearly everyone would look and smile with admiration. Many asked Mom where on earth she had purchased such warm, complete outfits. I became extremely confident, knowing that I looked magnificent in a city accustomed to the sight of pets sporting the latest canine fashions.

Mixed in with the joy, were several mentally uncomfortable nights. The first was the Following Saturday. Mom and Dad were invited to visit the president of his firm at his home in Montclair, New Jersey. I was accustomed to spending an evening alone now and then, but I was concerned about Dad driving such a distance, on highways slick with ice and snow. A predicted storm didn't help matters. I couldn't help but be anxious when they left in their rental car. After all, my racing imagination questioned, "What would happen to me if something happened to them?" Being in New York, 3,000 miles from home, added fuel to my concerns. A story kept running about in my head.

A few months before friends of my parents had been killed in a private plane crash and it was not until the following day that the relatives discovered their poodle, Mizzy in a cold house without food and water.

Finding a new home for her was tragic. She had been loved and pampered as I was; and I'm sure she was never happy again. All this was circling in my head when my parents locked the door and left. I didn't rest for a moment all the time they were gone. I paced the floor, and jumped for the door every time I heard a sound in the hallway.

In all honesty, I gave them until one o'clock to return. Those heartless people came in at four o'clock. I was out of my curly head with worry. I wept and howled until they felt terrible, which was how I wished them to feel. I never wanted that to happen to me again. They were worried about leaving me alone for so long and the next day, they waited on me like the poor and mistreated pet I was. They brought steaks and greenery to the suite and we ate dinner there.

Believe it or not, my folks left me again Monday night for dinner in Scarsdale. They promised they would not be late in returning, but it did little good. I knew I would worry until they were safely home. I did, but I only fussed and whined until midnight. Despite complaints, I was glad I had been in our warm suite. Mom informed me that it had been 12 degrees in Scarsdale; outside, it was a mere 2 degrees.

Mom and Dad seemed bent on desertion. After a day and a half of intensive mothering, Mom left me once again on Wednesday afternoon for lunch and a matinee performance of "Mame". Mom had wanted to see it for a long time so I tried hard not to blame her for going. But it made for a rotten dull day for me. Good old Dad returned at 2:00 p.m. and walked me, then stayed and played with me for an hour. Mom came home around 5:00. I must admit to how glad I was to see her. They say New York City is a lonely place, despite its millions of people and dogs; the loneliness somehow invaded our warm apartment and family group. I never remember clinging so hard to Mom and Dad.

The balance of our stay in New York was uneventful. I looked forward to our day of departure.

My clothing, despite its smartness, was beginning to be a literal drag. It became itchy to roll in the green grass under the occasionally hot sun. And I was sick of being alone almost every night. The folks included me in their cocktail parties, and I enjoyed them when I was fussed over properly by the guests. But this admiration was hollow, as they would all leave to have dinner at exciting places like "Toots Shores," "The Cattleman," "The Twenty-One

Chapter Five New York and a New Adventure

Club," and "Sardis." Glamorous places all, which I would never see despite my beauty. My folks always brought me lovely steaks and tasty roast beef, but you can, by now, understand how much I would have enjoyed attending these fabulous places, perhaps rubbing an elbow with a celebrity.

One night at Toots Shores, the President of the United States had dinner just a few tables down from my folks. How do humans do it?

Almost without exception they weren't as beautiful, well-mannered or affectionate as we poodles, who ate with dogs among dogs. How? why do they rate so well in the great "Chain of Being?" Well, I do digress, and I'm sorry-but I would like to have met the President and I'm sure he would have liked to have met me at a summit conference with myself, a French poodle with a Spanish name, living in the United States of America.

Chapter Six
Do They Put You in Chains?

Friday finally arrived. Down went another tranquilizer. Mom and Dad were intelligent people, but somehow they didn't connect my nervous frustration with those rotten pills and do the humane thing and flush them down the toilet. However, I was forced to swallow a pill two hours before flight time. At the airport I could feel the same nervous sensation I had experienced on our flight to New York. Mom walked me for several minutes before we boarded, giving me plenty of time to relieve myself and become drowsy. But when it was time to get into my bag I was so jumpy I cried. Mom, trying to soothe me, did not get into the plane until five minutes before take-off. As we made our way down the first- class section, intent on the less expensive seats in club coach, I cried out. See what those stupid pills made me do? Everything but what I should be doing-sleeping!

Mom and Dad settled themselves into their seats, put a blanket over my case and assumed a look of innocence. They were very apprehensive since my outburst, and becoming more so as I continued to whimper.

A minute later an agent appeared before our seat and asked Mom if she had a pet. I held my breath, wondering what her answer would be, also wondering about the fink who ratted on me. To be short and sweet, she was honest. He lectured her at length, saying that I was not permitted in the passenger section and I would have to be placed in the kennel, etc.., ad infinite, ad nausea. If I had had my boots on, I would have shaken in them.

We had a delayed departure. We were becoming infamous. Suddenly, another voice addressed the agent. It belonged to the senior stewardess. "Let me handle this," she told our tormentor. "I will take him up front of the first class section. He won't bother anyone." The agent was obviously relieved. Either he was a dog-lover at heart who had simply done his duty, or he hated dogs and was glad to have the problem taken from him. At any rate, he left the plane. I could hear people nattering about people like my parents who caused problems by not obeying the rules. I still want to believe there must have been very few dog-lovers on board who understood our problem.

The stewardess asked mom to come with her. Nervous, Mom took my case and followed her to the front of the first class section. She told Mom to keep me with her. I was so unhappy at the trouble I was causing Mom and Dad I wept, wondering what would happen next.

Soon, we were airborne. The stewardess came back and told my mother to take me out of the bag. I didn't know what to expect. But she was all smiles when I emerged. She was our saving angel. She was going to be our great friend!

This was my first look at the cabin of these machines I had flown in so many times. I was amazed at the room and activity. Across the aisle people played cards at a table. Two gentlemen seated there played gin rummy and watched eagerly when I emerged like Venus from the foam.

Both spoke up, saying there were glad to see what had caused all the commotion. By now I was finally getting dopey, but I tried to be charming to show my appreciation. Mom told them my name, which caused the usual round of comments. They asked my age, sex, and all the other standard questions, before wondering how anybody could object to something as handsome as me travelling in comfort. I was very grateful to these nice gentlemen for their attitude and compassion. Mom did not mention the fact that I had traveled over 40,000 miles by plane and that this was the first time we had ever encountered problems.

Well, no problems anymore. I was traveling in the lap of luxury, and puzzling how we might be able to do every trip. I curled up on Mom's lap and slept. My dreams were disturbed only by the stewardess serving drinks to Mom and the gentleman. Mom asked her if she would tell Dad that we were fine- more than fine, as a matter of fact. She said "I'll do better than that" and brought Dad up to sit with us. You should have heard Dad when he found Mom enjoying a scotch and water and me enjoying her lap. He was sure we were being confined in some closet for breaking the rules. He relaxed when the stewardess brought him a drink. We were all very happy and together again.

There was some kind of rule limiting the number of drinks served to passengers to only two. But since the rules had been broken, more got broken. We were served a third round and then a fourth. I think Mom and Dad could have flown home without a plane.

While they were blissfully becoming sauced, they were served creamed mushrooms on toast. The lovely fragrance disturbed me, so Mom gave me a taste. My palate was pleased.

When the stewardess noted my eager eyes and tongue, she brought a serving for me and another for Dad. I devoured every morsel. I thought it had been a lovely dinner. But then came soup, then a request to choose from three entrees: chicken,

Chapter Six Do They Put You in Chains?

lamb, or lobster. Dad took chicken and Mom had lobster. Wine came with the dinner, and then a desert tray was wheeled down the aisle, laden with French pastry. We made our selection. Mom selected a gooey piece with nuts, which I liked. The stewardess was afraid I wouldn't have enough so she added petit fours to each dish. Coffee was then served-and then after dinner drinks. I was a little worried because my folks never drank that much. But they kept their heads and did not neglect me for a minute. I just hoped they wouldn't neglect me on the long drive home.

After 4 hours, the pilot announced we were approaching the Los Angeles airport. No, we hadn't hitched onto a jet-stream. All the excitement, talking, and eating had made the time fly, and this was usually an intolerably long flight. Dad told the stewardess that he would retrieve the bags he had left in the other section. The stewardess said "Oh, no! The people back there think you're being punished. I'll go get your things." And she did.

I didn't make any fuss getting into my bag to deplane. Dad took down the stewardess' name and address and hosiery sizes. He planned to clad her limbs in free nylons in thanks for her help and wonderful attitude. Personally, I would have given her a lick (you know what I mean), but human beings don't do that. As it turned out, there was no driving involved when going home. Dad and Mom were very nervous about me when they boarded the Bonanza jet-prop flight to Palm Springs. We didn't receive attention on the flight, but then again, I didn't create another fuss that would demand attention.

The next week we flew to San Francisco. I could not forget how nice it had been flying home on Mom's lap. I made such a fuss in my bag that Mom finally inconspicuously sneaked me out and covered me with her fur, which was almost the same color as my fur.

I was smart enough to realize how annoyed they were with my behavior. They even threatened me with deportation to the pet compartment. That would have been like a descent into hell without Virgil or even a lousy golden bough for protection. I busily kissed her hand in apology and tried to peek at Dad to see if he were really serious, but I was drowned in fur. I pondered these events on that trip to San Francisco and convinced myself they wouldn't, they couldn't do that to me. However, when it was time to deplane, I didn't fight the bag. It was time to cooperate. All the way into San Francisco my parents discussed my future travel plans. They still sounded sincere in no longer taking me with them in the passenger section.

We were in San Francisco for a couple of days. The weather being strangely nice, we took long walks and romps. I loved the food at the St. Francis Hotel. My folks nearly always brought me prime ribs from the Medallion Room, with a lovely bone attached. I knew nearly all the help in the hotel and made it a point to be charming and appreciative so that I would always be welcomed.

Our trip home from San Francisco was short and I behaved fairly well. In Los Angeles, Dad picked up a rental car so that we could drive to Manhattan Beach to pick up a grandson ad his friend. They were to spend the weekend with us. Mom and Dad were pleased with my acquiescent behavior and I began to hope that I would be allowed to keep travelling with them. I enjoyed making them happy. Despite my occasional condescension to them, I was truly interested in pleasing them as much as they pleased me. The world should take a lesson from the harmony in our household.

We spent the weekend playing golf and entertaining the boys. I usually enjoy having my parents to myself, but Robin 12, and Greg,

Chapter Six Do They Put You in Chains?

13, were fine young men. They played with me a lot that weekend; tag, and other running games that take lots of energy. Mom liked to have someone give me a good workout once in a while. I also enjoyed having my picture taken. Such beauty deserved a multiplicity of images- and they took my picture over and over with their cameras which developed photos in minutes. But one photo made me look cross eyed, which made me cross. I must have moved my eyes the split-second the shutter snapped. I resented the photo and the way everyone laughed when they saw it. I tried several times to get my teeth into it, intending to make short work of the faulty image. They managed to keep it just out of my reach.

Otherwise, Mom and Dad had a lovely collection of snapshots of me, but I still wished for them to have my portrait done in oil. We had one of Mom in pastels that was just lovely, even though it made her look like it had been painted in oil, so I was understandably jealous. I was wishing for a more lasting monument of me than perishable snapshots would provide.

Dad's portrait prompted a few other remarks. We often wondered that as long as Mom looked younger in her portrait, why the artist didn't do the same for Dad by decorating his pate with hair. He was almost completely bald when I knew him, and even shaved off the slight fringe which still sprouted on the edge. Mom always told him he was very distinguished looking without hair. I suppose so. He was also a clean-looking man.

But I shouldn't be critical. Everyone could not be as fortunate as I was in appearance. All this is leading to something I want to be definite about. I really loved Dad. He could not have been nicer to me. I realize the adjustments he had to make when I entered the household. Being the type of man referred to as 'macho' he had made fun of people, especially men, walking their poodles. But he did not allow assumptions about masculinity to rule his feelings about me.

I remember that when we stayed at hotels, it was Dad who jumped out of a comfortable bed to take me on a walk so that I could be comfortable. He even talked to me when we rode the elevators, uncaring as to what people thought. But he wasn't entirely altruistic in overcoming his embarrassment; he liked the fuss people made over me, especially by women and girls. He once remarked that if he were ever reincarnated, he intended to come back as a poodle.

He meant the remark to be a compliment; and I took it as such. Our travels resumed the following week. I made Mom and Dad even happier with my reformed behavior. We drove into Los Angeles and checked into the Century Plaza Hotel after business was done. My folks left only enough time to eat in the Granada Room. The next day we went to Long Beach on more business, and then proceeded to the airport.

Our flight to Denver was pure pleasure, at least to Mom and Dad. For once, they weren't concerned over my illegal presence, for they had secured pet permission from the airlines. I still would have preferred flying outside the bag, but knew I would be coldly ignored if I fussed. I settled down and slept most of the trip. We flew into a Denver which was warmer than it should have been, but comfortable in its unseasonable heat.

There was the usual round of business, lunches, and enjoyable times. I sometimes wonder what the folks had done on their business trips when they did not have me to worry about. We then flew back to Los Angeles via Continental. All secure once more with pet permission, we enjoyed the flight, not fearful of discovery. Again I ask, what did people have against this handsome fellow, namely me?

Chapter Six Do They Put You in Chains?

I accepted this strange prejudice, and then came close to not accepting it when it struck me how unfair it was to me and my brethren. Only sophisticated enough not to fuss about pets, but they still had to remained bagged. And ever since the flight from New York, I resented being confined.

But I did finally have my way, and delightfully, the airlines were responsible for my new freedom. A new ruling had gone into effect all carry-on luggage must fit under the seat, in order to keep the floor clear in case of emergency evacuation. If my bag was pushed under the seat, I would be unable to breathe. So thereafter, when we boarded a plane, as soon as Mom sat down, she sneaked me up beside her on the seat. I was then concealed by her fur. It was a little warm, but far more comfortable than staying in the bag. I was fortunate that Mom did not even qualify as plump. And I think people always wondered why she carried that fur.

Things proceeded smoothly in this fashion for a while. But one week, rather than flying home to Los Angeles from San Francisco, we hopped to Phoenix. I was my usual charming, quiet self on these flights, snuggled up next to Mom. But the flight to Palm Springs from Phoenix was indeed another affair.

The only airline with direct service from Phoenix to Palm Springs was Bonanza, a small airline with correspondingly small planes, with likewise small seats. They were so narrow that not even one average-sized person could sit comfortably, much less with a poodle sitting alongside. I wondered how they would meet and resolve this wrinkle, confident they would think of something. Dad did: I would have to ride in the luggage compartment. When I heard this, I sulked all day. I had not traveled separately with my parents since that disastrous experience between Phoenix and Denver years before.

Dad boarded early to hold seats. Mom waited with me until about three minutes before flight time. She then personally checked on my location, which was a compartment just behind the cockpit. It was filled with luggage that was held in place by a heavy net. Mom was worried that my bag would turn over and suffocate me. The pilot finally opened the door to the cock pit and told her to put my bag just outside his door so that he could keep an eye on me. This was nice of him, but I daresay his humanitarianism or dogitarianism was motivated by the desire to get the plane off the ground. Mom was relieved by his offer, and so was I.

Up until now I was silent. I wasn't being Good, I was petrified. But then I heard a reassuring voice. The door at the other end of the luggage compartment had been opened by the stewardess, and there was my dear Dad sitting right next to the door. He told the stewardess to take good care of me. Then the door was closed and we readied for takeoff. What happened next is quite amusing.

Just before we were airborne, the co-pilot opened the door, took my bag and placed me between he and the pilot. Things would have been all right; however, things went wrong and Murphy's rule prevailed. While in flight, Mom always opened the side zipper of my bag so that I could have more air. She had told the attendant to open the zipper but this had not been done. I couldn't stand it. I put my teeth into the material around the air holes and with strength I didn't know I had, I ripped a hole five inches wide. It was laughably easy for me to escape.

The pilot and co-pilot were very busy taking the plane up during my struggle. When they leveled the plane out and relaxed, you can imagine their surprise when they found a handsome poodle between them.

After the first shock, the pilot tried to

return me to bag, but realized it was so badly damaged that it would not confine me. I was expecting torture, but the good man took me on his lap, rubbed my back and talked to me for the entire flight to Palm Springs.

I had not intended to be a problem, but then again, I am sure you understand my situation. And wouldn't my poodle mother have been impressed if she had known about this adventure!

When we arrived in Palm Springs the pilot placed me back in my bag and carried me off the plane. When they saw the pilot doing the honors, with my curly head poking out, their mouths flew open. Nothing, however, came out. They were so upset, they failed to get the co-pilot's name. Their thanks were so garbled; I really wasn't too proud of their behavior.

That little episode made it impossible to use the plaid bag, so Mom dusted off the old black one, stitched a new fishnet stocking around the air-holes, put in a new pad and we were ready for new adventures. I heard Mom tell Dad that she was not about to buy another bag until she saw how I was going to behave. If I had been able to communicate I would have told her that I had no intention of staying in that bag from then on. One has to put one's paw down.

I proved my determination on a trip to Seattle the following week. I was very good on the plane, even though I made a couple of small noises to warn her. As soon as we were settled in our seats, I whimpered and rocked the bag. Mom wasted no time sneaking me up beside her. I was very good on that flight and very good from then on. I liked traveling in the seat beside her, even if I was quite warm under her wrap. Paris is famed for its diplomacy, and I would have proved my ancestral city proud of its canine son for my gentle tact sharpened with thorough determination.

Chapter Seven
I Thought I Was Going to Die

We were in San Francisco again. Our new arrangements on airline flights were becoming routine. I no longer stayed in that hateful bag. I tolerated it long enough to board the plane and then disembark. During the flight, I happily slept next to Mom. Dad marveled at how clever Mom was getting me into and out of the bag. She was so fast that even he sometimes missed the action. As the first winter of this new arrangement waned, I grew concerned at how she would conceal me in warm weather. After all, you can't drag a fur coat onto a plane in the middle of summer without somebody noticing. She spoke of carrying a wool sweater, but worried about my being allergic. Sneezes are pretty obvious to a flight attendant.

We were soon in San Francisco again. We had gone up the Bay to Walnut Creek for a day's work, but returned to our favorite haunt, the St. Francis, that night. Mom had several packages to carry as well as leading me. We got to our room and she left some of the packages at the door after opening it. Placing her coat and me on the bed, she stepped out to get the packages, as I jumped off the bed to follow her. I was jerked back.

Somehow I had caught my back right leg (the one that had been operated on) in the clasp of the leash. I screamed and then choked as my

Chapter Seven I Thought I Was Going to Die

neck and leg were snapped together.

Mom was cool under fire-and she swung into action. She could not free my leg but managed to unhook my collar. I gasped at air, but my leg felt as though it were caught in a bear trap. I used my breath to scream. A maid came running in; she had heard me all the way at the end of the corridor. With her help Mom managed to free my leg.

We collapsed into wrecks. Mom shook from strain, I trembled with pain. Dad then sailed in on this crisis. He had been parking the car. He was sorry for what had happened, but I don't think he had any idea what we had been through. I understood his lack of concern, but I clung to Mom for the rest of the evening. What would I have done without her? What would she have done without me?

Our next round of travel took us to Los Angeles, Santa Ana and La Jolla. In the last city, we expected to stay at the Beach and Tennis Club until Dad. However, he noticed the dreadful sign: No Pets in the Rooms. But Mom simply sneaked me in. All would have been well except I would be denied the run of the place. As it turned out, I was disappointed beyond disappointment for rain began to fall in pitchforks (whatever those are). I didn't mind the wetness, but I do become most un-lovely when it rains.

The next day was California-pleasant. Dad spent a lot of time with me and I even went into the store several times to visit Mom. We then flew to Phoenix in the late afternoon. We went first-class so I had ample room in the seat beside Mom. (I Told you I was a first-class dog-they often joked about how I had classed up their act, and I did, but really they deserved first class as much as I did.) Mom, by the way, was now carrying a summer-weight white sweater to cover me. I swear, the two of us could have made a living on the magic circuit doing hand tricks. She would take my bag on her lap, unzip it and out I slid under her sweater. Dad was always a nervous wreck until we were all settled and the bag was under the seat. Of course, he went through it again when we prepared to land.

This particular journey was a little different. We left Phoenix (where I always received a proper welcome at the *Townhouse*) before we flew to Salt Lake. Dad had been informed the last time we were there that I would no longer be welcomed at the Utah Hotel. He demanded to see the manager. He was a nice person as it turned out, and told Dad that although they were officially barring all pets, I was to be an exception. (Did that ever make me feel like a big deal!)

But even though I was an exception, we were still asked (but politely, I must add) to use the freight elevator, which was in back of the passenger elevator. The manager hastened to explain that this was not degradation; it was to insure that the operators and other guests would not be aware of my presence.

I was naturally a little hurt, but a nice elderly man operated the back elevator and I soon decided I liked it even better than the fancy automated job that served the lobby. Mom and Dad rode it too-and if was good enough for them, it was good enough for me.

After the usual business in the stores, we drove ninety miles to Logan the next day, to attend a wedding reception for one of Mom's nephews. We were unable to attend the wedding. My enforced absence was due to the fact that I was a dog. Mom and Dad's absence arose from the fact that unless you are married in Mormon Temple, you cannot attend a Temple wedding. So they proceeded to Mom's sister's house for the time being. There were eighteen people in all, plus the most attractive little girl poodle named Tiffy. I spent the whole afternoon romancing her. She seemed to like me, but failed to return my affection. It was still a great afternoon, and we ran and played and smooched until I was a nervous wreck.

My parents could attend the reception, which was held in the recreation hall of the church. I was glad to be taken along, but gladder when I learned I had to stay in the car. For once, I welcomed the previously disliked alone time in order to sleep quietly.

The folks did not stay too long at the reception and we left almost immediately for Salt Lake. It took me two days to recover from my romp with Tiffy. We returned to Palm Springs the next day. Under the desert sun I slept for two days, weary of the world. Sophistication can be tiring!

Chapter Eight
Yet Another Cliff Hanger

Travel is interesting, at times fascinating, but, if constant, it becomes routine.

Routine enough not to sacrifice my reader's interest to endless minutiae about planes and hotels. But, occasionally, the routine was broken by interesting, sometimes tragic events.

By this time, I had turned two years old. We were in our usual round of the Magnin stores in Seattle, Portland, San Francisco, Oakland and Palo Alto. Our flight to Seattle was as prosaic as was the short flight to Portland. However, the flight to San Francisco, was a hair-raiser. And with a poodle, a hair-raiser can be a painful, and unforgettable experience.

As usual, Mom sneaked me on board, out of my bag and settled me down beside her. Suddenly, we heard the captain's very urgent voice: "All passengers leave the plane immediately with all personal belongings." He repeated the message twice. Mom frantically grabbed me and my case and tried to put us in proper order. She had been reading a newspaper and in her excitement pushed part of the paper into the bag with me. She pulled me and the paper out, threw the paper on the floor and stuffed me in again, this time tangling me with the sweater. On the third attempt she succeeded getting me in and closing the bag. I would have surely been discovered but for the fact that all the other passengers were too excited and busy collecting their own belongings to witness our struggle.

On leaving the plane, we were confined to the boarding area. Mom asked permission to go the ladies room, but was told to stay put. She was scared because I was helplessly moving around in the bag, my highly strung nerves unstrung.

He soon found out that thirty-three army recruits were among the passengers and one of them was a hippie with the usual long hair and barefoot. When he passed the agent, he remarked they would never get him to San Francisco, as he planned to blow the plane up. Naturally the agent hastened to report it and the brown-wrapped package he had been carrying. This might have been his laundry, but after that stupid declaration, who was going to trust him? For our sake, I'm glad the airline took him seriously.

To conclude this unpleasant adventure, they marched the recruits to a separate place and arrested the idiot, which just might have been what he wanted. In the meantime, they checked the plane for bombs. We had no idea how long we would be detained, and I was getting very warm and very nervous in the bag. I let Mom know how uncomfortable I was by crying softly several times. She finally got permission to go to the lady's room. She took me out, gave me a drink and I felt much better. Then the loud speaker spoke loudly: "Mrs. Baker, please return to the boarding area." How we started. If I had been able to sweat, I would have done so. We hurried out.

Dear old Dad, he had done it again! Right across from the boarding area where we waited, Dad found a flight leaving for San Francisco. He had obtained seats, but not luggage transfer. This was the least of our worries. In seconds, we had boarded the other plane and were comfortably seated. I was very fortunate to have a human Dad with-what do you call it-"sprezzaturra." This is the art of doing difficult things with ease and grace. He always managed to solve our problems easily, without too much discomfort for me.

We were overwrought for the first part of the flight, but after Mom and Dad had cocktails, and I licked some ice, we felt better. Soon we were in our favorite room at the St. Francis.

The next day Mom and Dad worked the San Francisco store. I was so tired from the ridiculous excitement of the day before I didn't mind being left alone. I also had a sore spot next to my tail. I thought Mom had accidentally pinched it in our little wild adventure on the plane. But Thursday I felt worse.

Dad walked me that morning and after returning to the room, remarked to Mom that I was acting strangely. She promptly checked me over and found a lump half the size of a walnut right next to my tail. She was very upset; I was not too far behind her in emotion. Dad wasn't happy either. When she discovered I had a temperature, her worry became distress. Again, I was not too far behind. They had a meeting at the Oakland store at 9:00. Hot and drowsy, I slept on the pillow placed between them in the rental car. I didn't mind at the time and still don't mind that they tended to business after making such a frightening discovery.

For one thing, I felt too awful, to care. But I also realized that they were humans. They had to work for their living, unlike we canine 'lilies of the field'. If worry could be considered the gauge of their love, they adored me. I knew I was not off their minds for a moment that morning.

Rather than leaving me in the car, Mom took me in her arms and carried me right into the store. Everybody was concerned when they learned of my illness and made every effort to make me

CHAPTER EIGHT YET ANOTHER CLIFF HANGER

comfortable. I was too dopey to react to all the attention I would have normally eaten up before asking for seconds. After the meeting, Dad called his sister, who lived in Piedmont. She owned a poodle, so she knew of an excellent doctor. She called him and made an appointment, met us and led us to the hospital. I will always be grateful that she went beyond the call of duty to see to my aid.

The strange doctor discovered I had a clogged anal gland, which had ulcerated. Frankly, I was being poisoned, and ironically, by my own body. I listened to all this with some wonder, for I did not even know I had anal glands. The doctor explained to Mom and Dad that these glands were like the human appendix; that is, no longer necessary to the body's functioning.

Thousands of years ago, dogs secreted an odor from them, much as a skunk does, but of course, not as obnoxious an odor. A complex process called 'evolution' had gradually shut these glands down as they were no longer needed by the dog as a method of survival. But they still continued to partially function, and we were told that the people at the Poodle Parlor should have expelled the fluid when grooming me. Because they had not, my gland had closed, and it was angrily demanding to be re-opened.

The doctor told me he must operate immediately. He also wanted to keep me overnight; perhaps for a couple of days. My parents declared this impossible as they were due in Palo Alto the next morning. The doctor fought them long enough to give in. He said they could pick me up at 4:00 P.M., if all went well. Mother would have to be my nurse, bathing my wound at night and in the morning. I would have preferred my mother's care over the tender mercies of strangers, but I have these thoughts now. Right then, I was so sick that all I wanted was for the doctor to start operating. I didn't shake or cry when Mom and Dad left. I was glad to see them go, because I didn't want to add to their misery. I heard the doctor telling Dad he would call him about 2:00 with a progress report. Poor Mom and Dad returned to their work, with their minds far from their tasks. An assistant gave me a shot of something, and suddenly Mom and Dad were picking me up. I found out later that Dad had called at 2:00, and the doctor told him he had had to make a larger incision that he anticipated. I would require a great deal of care. Mom and Dad didn't mind for they were so relieved at my restored health. However, they were totally unprepared for the way I looked when they picked me up. At 4:00 I was still only half-conscious. I couldn't stand up by myself and my beautiful curls were wet and matted from the water used to clean away the blood. My bottom was an equal mess; there was a gash an inch and a half long next to my tail. Blood and just plain goop oozed out. If I had felt better, my lack of fastidiousness would have revolted me.

Through the fog I heard the doctor apologizing for my appearance. But Mom didn't care about that; her tenderness was fired by my awful looks. At the moment, pain was held off on my numbness. They were very gentle with me as they carried me to the car and placed me in the travel bag, all padded with towels. Dad then shopped for the necessary drugs and we were finally on our way to Palo Alto and the Cabana Inn. I do not remember much about the ride or the next two days for that matter. I do remember being thirsty, which Mom and Dad slaked by a little ice water. My incision was bathed and a pill would go down my throat.

They worked in the Palo Alto store until Friday noon of that endless week. We were finally on our way home, but that posed trouble. Dad tried and tried to gain permission from our airline to extend pet permission so that I would not have to hide.

Chapter Eight Yet Another Cliff Hanger

Those heartless wretches would not relent. Now what? I was still too sick to care very much at the time, though I felt more indignant than usual over the airlines' unreasoning hatred for dogs. Being staffed by human beings, which automatically made the majority of them dog owners, you would think they would realize that dogs are often better behaved than children. Mom and Dad decided to do something they never did: drive home to Palm Springs, which was a ten-hour journey. I am touched to think they loved me enough to make that terrible drive which came at the end of an exhausting week of hard work and worry. The people at the store were very understanding when we left Palo Alto at 1:30 instead of 5:00 to start the long drive. Mom and Dad often stopped to take me out of the car.

I was also getting hungry again. Mom and Dad had offered bites of meat, but I couldn't stomach it. At this particular stop, Dad bought himself and Mom milkshakes. The moment Mom started to drink hers, I perked up. She let me take a drop or two from her fingers. When she saw how eagerly I licked the milkshake away, she poured some in a dish. After drinking about one-third of her shake, I felt better and slept for a long time. Mom and Dad began to relax.

They took turns driving to Palm Springs so they would not get sleepy. Along the long road home, they called our oldest family who were spending the week in our home. They waited up for us. Missy, their pretty Sheltie, was sympathetic. She sniffed my incision and cried over my lameness. She did not rough me up with a romp, which is her usual method of greeting me. We were soon in bed after our arrival.

I slept apart from Mom and Dad so they wouldn't hurt me during the night. The next morning, I felt much better and could even raise my leg in the time-honored position when Dad took me for my morning walk. I hardly felt any discomfort when Mom bathed my incision. I was healing rapidly. The family left Sunday evening and Monday morning we drove to Los Angeles. Fortunately, that week most of our business was within driving distance, eliminating wrangles with the airlines. The week itself was uneventful; Mom and Dad and I had lots of time to sleep. As I recovered, I was increasing in need of grooming. My periodic beauty treatments had been postponed and my hair was getting long. I looked like a hippie.

I enjoyed being well groomed, and enjoyed even more the compliments people paid me on my immaculate appearance. Mom did her best trimming around my eyes and ears, but the rest of my coat was pretty ragged.

Once back in town, Mom tried to get an appointment at the parlor but they were completely booked. Mom and Dad didn't trust me with just any operator. I was glad for their discretion, for some of my friends had been gashed by careless cads. So I went a week without being properly groomed. By then, I was well enough to be disgusted at my appearance.

Chapter Nine
Mom's Unsavory Uncles

The following week, we drove to Phoenix, the site of the last Magnin trip of that spring tour. I was glad the current round of travels was soon to be over because Mom was able to spend more time with me.

We drove to Tucson in order for Dad to work at Levy's and then we drove back north to Carefree, a new development twenty miles north of Scottsdale, nestled away from the mountains, away from everything but comfort.

Our room at the hotel was mammoth. It had enormous beds, sofa, table, chairs and refrigerator to match. There was also a grassy patio where I could play and roll. Mom gave me a prime rib bone all covered with juicy meat, which I enjoyed while she and Dad had cocktails. It was still daylight when they left for dinner, leaving me behind tired out from gnawing my bone.

When they returned, they had postcards of the restaurant they had eaten in. While I looked them over, I listened to them describe the place, which was called Pinnacle Peak Patio. A Stork Club it was not. It sat all by itself about seventeen miles from Carefree, making up in atmosphere what it lacked in sophistication. The only meal served was a two-pound porterhouse steak, with salad and cowboy beans. The back a portion of their steaks were more five or six dogs my size could not have eaten at one time. This was all rather disconcerting to this tiny poodle.

As befitting its location, Pinnacle Peak was also very carefree in its dress. They insisted on "carefreeness". If a man arrived wearing a necktie, one of the waitresses cut if off and tossed it over a rafter. They showed me a picture of this spectacle; the restaurant looked like a cave, with little stalactites hanging from the ceiling. I'm sorry I did not see the place for myself, although it sounded a little overwhelming. They promised to show it to me sometimes, and I was pleased for the postcards.

The next morning, we drove out onto the desert. Mom wished to find a mine that two of her uncles had owned. When she was a small girl, she had vacationed there, but things had changed so much she could not locate it. Dad teased her that her wish was going to shake the car apart as a result of driving many miles on a rocky road that day. I didn't mind the bumps, but the dust made me sneeze. The trip was somewhat enjoyable and Mom told us about her uncles. I had never heard about her pedigree, so I was quite interested. She told of one incident of her father, brother and her taking her up to the mine in an open Ford, so that her uncles could have fresh milk. She and her brother had to hold the goat by the tail and neck to keep it from jumping out. And it was no easy task hanging onto a goat's tail, she assured us. Frankly, I could not imagine how they managed with those primitive vehicles she spoke about: no air conditioning, no windows, narrow tires always going flat. I'm glad it was before my time.

It seems her uncles did other things than mining. In those days, in Arizona, there was a law called 'prohibition' which curtailed the sale and use of alcoholic beverages. The legislature must have been insane to pass a law like that. The best, most moderate of human beings like to have a drink, so you can imagine the rumpus that ensued when drinking was made illegal. Anyway, her two uncles owned and operated a saloon before the law went into effect. At the mine, during their spare time, they distilled a drink called "white Mule" evidently similar to alcohol. Mom said it was much in demand by doctors and incidentally, by anyone else who could get their hands on it. Those two jokers-pardon me, Mom's uncles, simply went under cover for the duration of prohibition. And they knew what they were doing-at least, they were in a business that they understood. After all, Mom said, they had to make a living. Their operation was illegal, but it was stimulating (no pun intended!)

Mom, at this point, was rationalizing, trying to make an illegal activity sound legal by considering it within the boundaries of circumstances. Their operation was illegal alright. Their integrity was questionable. I thought this and felt quite self-righteous, until I recalled that I eagerly participated in clandestine airplane rides.

But I had to stay with my parents. And I was so unhappy in the pet compartment. And, after all, I thought, in five, ten, twenty years, who would care that a poodle was where it should not have been?

Then a strange, grim thought struck me: I would

not be with my parents forever. I had developed an imperfect understanding of a universal destroyer called 'death' that would visit me someday. Good heavens, I thought. What then? What then?

I made myself forget about it and concentrated on the pleasures at hand.

We drove back to Palm Springs, arriving in the late afternoon. Dad and Mom spent a couple of hours cleaning the place up, and then Mom, tried to make an appointment to get me cleaned up.

The first opening was the next Friday, which was Good Friday. I was getting more awful looking by the day, but Mom never traveled the week before Easter, another Christian celebration that I didn't quite understand, other than it had to do with the death of the child born on Christmas.

Anyway, my appearance was not too important that week and I even swam, although I emerged from the pool looking like a drowned rat.

Although I wasn't going out to see people, people came in to see me. The oldest family soon arrived to spend Easter on the desert. Our middle family usually came, but this year went to Salt Lake instead. I was well enough to romp with Missy again. She was big enough to byte me in half if she wished to, but then again, why should she have wanted to do such a terrible thing? And she was a gentle girl and always careful not to hurt me.

One of her favorite tricks was to run, make a fast turn and then stop. This was made funny by me being directly behind her. When she pivoted, I always smacked into her, head over heels. Bless her heart! But that Easter she let me outrun her every time. She was making sure I did not hurt myself.

This family was devoted to pets too. Greg, the youngest son, had saved his money and bought a masked, wooly beast called a raccoon. Why he did such a thing I can't fathom, when he could have bought a poodle! When Morgan-the raccoon was little, he was cute but this Easter he was grown and weighed over 60 pounds. He was further weighted down by a rotten disposition.

When Ric, the oldest son tried to give him a drink, Morgan bit the hand that watered him, all the way through the meat between his thumb and forefinger. Before that, I empathized with Morgan, for he was mostly confined to a cage. I had even tried talking to him through the cage wires. After this terrible display of temper, I stayed away. My tender hide didn't need any more scars, particularly one inflicted by Morgan's needle-sharp teeth.

Perhaps I'm being unfair to judge Morgan so harshly, for I am measuring his personality against a dog's sunny disposition. And raccoons are nocturnal animals, so he had to mold his instincts to human life. I understood that in the summer, when he accompanied the family to the mountains, his disposition improved considerably. Mom and Dad talked about visiting their eldest family in the mountains in the coming summer. I hoped that Morgan and I would arrive at some sort of truce so we could at least tolerate each other.

A strange thing began to happen to me. This was truly strange, for I showed signs of becoming apricot again. My mother was very pleased, claiming I would be easier to care for. She was very fussy over my appearance, which made me glad, but her very tired.

As though touched by Midas, I began to become golden. The color started at the base of my tail and crept down my back. Before, I was silvery in appearance, now I was gilded. Oh well, I thought. Gold is more valuable than silver, and I very doubted for a moment Mom would not take excellent care of my new golden coat.

Chapter Ten
I Meet the Youngest Family

My life was filled with interesting events; some were to my liking, others were not. But at least life was never dull. I'm still trying to figure out the exact meaning of "It's a dog's life."

One spring we made our usual trip to New York. The events which happened during the visit and after the visit were very unusual. As always we stayed at the only home I ever had in New York, Ten Park Avenue. I soon found out that our youngest family would come to New York to visit us. Daddy John was a graduate of West Point and was a career officer. They had returned from a two-year assignment in Turkey (I didn't know where that was, but it sounded delicious!)

They were now stationed at Otis AFB in Massachusetts. Before I had been adopted by Mom and Dad, they had made a trip to Europe and had spent several days with this family in

Chapter Ten I Meet the Youngest Family

Adana, Turkey. The experience was a highlight in their lives. The previous November, just a few days after their return to the States we had gone to Massachusetts for a brief visit.

We were only with them overnight but the experience was a pleasant one and I had found all the children to be very nice. They treated me with love and consideration which I expected and deserved. The experience was a pleasant one, so I anticipated, rather than dreaded, their visit to us in New York.

They arrived: Ty, three; Diane, five; Joanie, seven; Cathy, nine; and of course Daddy; John and Mommy; Pat. We all greeted each joyfully. I was glad to have young people around who had enough energy to play. Mom and Dad were fine at home but I was fortunate to get one good walk when I'm in New York. We all had a nice afternoon and welcomed the chance to nap while they went to dinner. I did grow jealous when they returned,

as I learned that they all walked down Fifth Avenue, and ascended to the top of the Empire State Building. I had never been there.

Jealousy became apprehension. The next morning I learned That Two of the daughters were coming back to Palm Spring with us. This news really took the curl out of my hair. It was one thing to have a short visit from the grandchildren, but to have a couple of them living and travelling with us, distressed me.

Before you groan at my selfishness, I wish to point out that I am after all a dog. And like all dogs, my parents are my universe. I was so annoyed over being displaced I crawled under the bed and stayed there until time to leave. I sulked all the way to the airport. The rest of the family started back to Massachusetts, minus the two children we had inherited.

Cathy and Joanie were very excited about going

home with us and tried very hard to get me to join in with their pleasure. I remained aloof to their blandishments all the way to the coast. I remember hearing Cathy telling Joanie that she thought I hid under the sweater to avoid them.

Dad rented a car and we drove to Palm Springs. By now, I was softening because frankly, I'm made of butter. The girls did everything they could to please me and I began to realize that they both presented a chance for more attention ... strenuous attention, the kind dogs need. Mom and Dad loved me petted me and occasionally played ball with me, but they weren't particularly fleet of foot and I did love a good romp in the grass.

Each evening when we were home they would run and chase me until I cried "uncle," or at least barked an equivalent expression. When I was exhausted they would find their jump ropes and spend another hour whirling it over and under their head and feet. It seemed to give them great pleasure. They tried to get me interested in learning to jump with them but one tries and I gave up. The rope just whipped my legs out from under me. One thing I never did enjoy, was being laughed at.

And I wasn't displaced, at least unduly. My place in the car was still on the pillow, between them. Cathy and Joanie sat in the back. Dad put a chaise lounge pad in the rear of the station wagon so the girls could take turns stretching out for a nap when we took our usual business trips. We traveled quite a bit together. And when we were in Phoenix, staying at Del Webb's Townhouse, I learned that I was still number one in Moms heart.

She would allow the girls to swim in the hotels pool, but not me. She was scared that I might 'catch something'. She didn't worry about Cathy and Joanie's health!

While in Phoenix, Mom and Dad took the girls to the Pinnacle Peak Patio, which they had

Chapter Ten I Meet the Youngest Family

enjoyed so much the year before. As usual, I didn't go, but I was worn out from a game of ball, and later comforted by a wonderful piece of steak. The girls had bought some souvenirs for themselves and their family. Joanie had a little donkey about six inches high, which was covered with fur-like skin. She named him "Jack the Ass,' and placed him on the table next to her pillow so she could see him when she opened her eyes.

I was a little hurt that Mom hadn't bought one for me, she knew how much I liked toy animals. After everyone had fallen asleep, I stood up on my hind legs, took Jack the Ass and played with him. I didn't mean to harm the toy or upset anyone, but I suppose I did get carried away on occasion. I chewed and licked, and then fell asleep with Jack between my paws, and my chin on his back.

I was totally unprepared for the reaction my little nocturnal activity would have the next morning. Joanie awoke to not find Jack on the table. When she found him on the floor, a tornado began. I still maintain that Jack was not in that bad of shape-just a little fur was taken from his back and his ribbon slightly mangled. But it would have taken buckets to hold Joanie's tears. She cried and cried. I had never seen anything equal to that deluge. Thank goodness, Mom didn't scold me. In her wisdom, she understood that I did not intend to do any harm. She finally got control of Joanie's tears by promising her that Jack would be as good as new with a little glue and a new ribbon.

Later that morning we went shopping for the tools of Jack's repair. After buying glue, ribbon, needle and thread, Joanie insisted that Mom buy a toy for me. I wondered if she wished to apologize for the fuss she had made and the black thoughts she had obviously had of me, or if she wanted to keep her toy safe from my teeth.

They found a small monkey with the bright

orange fur that was to my liking. I licked Joanie's hand and face to show my appreciation. She kissed me and rubbed my tummy to prove that there were no hard feelings. Mom plied her needle magic on Joanie's toy and soon he was like new. I liked the yellow ribbon better than the original pink one. The girls agreed with me.

When Jack was patched up, he was then placed beyond my reach. I was a little hurt by this, because I had no intention of repeating my nocturnal affair with him, but I had no way of letting them know this. A girl's tears are something I can't stand. And for all my pooh-poohing of Joanie's tears, I realized it was a pretty rotten thing I did.

That toy meant a lot to her. I know that wherever she is now, she probably remembers that incident with some embarrassment, which she shouldn't. A child's love for a toy is an innocent and wonderful thing.

Our stay in Phoenix, despite this fiasco, was very pleasant. Their entire stay with us was enjoyable. Mom made sure they had the fun they should have had. I was usually included on their romps, except when they went to Disneyland and the zoo.

In fact, Mom didn't even ask me if I would like to go, which distressed me and then later relieved me, after I heard about the scary rides at Disneyland. The scary rides would have insulted my sensitive stomach. I also realized that the Zoo was not the place for me either. When the girls told me about the size of some of those animals, I began shaking.

While they were here, Ric, the eldest son of the oldest family was nice enough to take them to these places. He came to play golf with his grandfather, but he was a Disneyland junkie and probably knew the park better than Walt and Mickey combined. We all had a good time when he visited.

In all, the two months the girls spent with us

Chapter Ten I Meet the Youngest Family

were very nice. A couple of weeks had to pass before I got over the habit of going into their room each night to kiss them and spend an hour at the foot of their bed. I missed the sound of the voices and the evening games. But I did get back the extra attention Mom and Dad always showered on me before the visit from the girls. I had found out that rain always brings the flowers.

Chapter Eleven
More Health Problems

Every summer I received a kind of shot to make me immune to the many different diseases dogs are susceptible. Every two years I had a rabies shot. When it came time for the latter, Mom made an appointment with Dr. Jackson. The morning of our visit, she brushed me and discovered what I already began to suspect: my other anal gland was acting up. I had quite a lump on the right side of my tail. When Dr. Jackson inspected my derriere he confirmed Mom's fears. But the going was easier this time: a shot of antibiotic and some pills soothed her fears for a day, while we waited to see what the abscessed gland would do. He hoped to avoid surgery, which echoed my sentiments. I spent that day in a sleepy, miserable condition and spent the night in pain. Mom tried some hot packs to see if they could relieve me. She and Dad held me and placed hot wash cloths against my aching rear until I was quite comfortable. Ah, how they loved me! Not only could they parade me down a street in all my glory, they could also stick by me when there were unpleasant, downright disgusting things to do.

I was resting in the early morning hours when the abscess broke and drained. Mom hurried me to Dr. Jackson who told her the hot packs had been the right thing to do. He checked my temperature, found it normal and instructed Mom to keep giving me the pills. In a few days I was my normal self and the next Saturday I got my booster and rabies shot which had been held off. Dad then renewed my license. They worried when my license was not up to date, because they feared I would be lost. An old license dangling about my neck would make it look as if nobody cared. I wish I could have told them to stop worrying. I never planned on straying too far from home or from Mom and Dad.

Something funny was in the air, and it wasn't my tail. I overheard some phone conversations between Mom and my poodle mother's mother, which made it sound as though we were soon to visit her. When I looked quizzically at her, Mom picked me up and loved me, which was a clue to my future, I daresay.

I had recently taken up with a very sweet little lady poodle. Mom called her 'Baby'. She was brownish black, and about my size. She was very young and when we were home she ran across the fairway to pay us a visit each evening. We all liked her very much and I didn't object to the attention she sneaked away from my folks.

One night, as we took our usual walk around the block after dinner, we passed by a house. Baby was on the lawn, playing with her young master. Mom asked the boy what the poodle's name was: 'suzette`. I was very pleased. She fitted her true name. We had walked on a bit when Suzette came trotting after us. A little bold of her perhaps, but nice. When we returned to our house, Dad took us both to the back yard where we had a good run in the grass. She was fast and a little rough. One of her favorite tricks was to run as fast she could, pivot on the well-worn dime and hit me right in the middle. She had probably been taking lessons from Missy. I forever tried to anticipate this maneuver and never quite could. But I did enjoy our romps together and hoped that she would escort us in our walks.

One joyful experience; now becomes a traumatic one. Dad disappeared. Of course, he didn't vanish-but he went to a human hospital for a hernia operation. I didn't quite understand what was taking place, and why he didn't come home nights. I knew that he was undergoing a process that I had undergone at the vets, but I was always brought home immediately. And to make it worse, Mom spent most of the time at the hospital every day and did not come home until late at night. I was very lonely. As usual, I derived some benefit from the situation! I had half of the king-size bed all to myself. I spent a lot of time curled up on it, happy in my parents' lingering odor. But for a poodle who had been forever in the security of two loving parents, it was a terrible time. Finally, Dad's absence got to me. Each time Mom left me I was sure she wouldn't return. My happy welcomes became hysterical occasions.

One day, Mom left the home in good spirits. She returned in even better spirits for dear old Dad was with her. I was so happy to see him I cried and kissed him until I was even more exhausted than he. For several days Dad was not much fun. He didn't even leave the house. Then, the third or fourth day, he awoke in great spirits. He took my leash from the hook and out we went for a walk, just like the old times. He still couldn't come swimming with us, but the lovely walks made me happy enough.

Chapter Twelve
The Ho! Ho! Season —Again

Again, the jolly season was upon us. The middle family had spent Thanksgiving with us, and I had been very disappointed for they had not brought Mimi. Conversation suggested something about that cute lady getting mixed up with some fellow from the streets.

Mixed up indeed-she had had five puppies! I understood that the family kept one. Suzy was petting me one day when she said to Mom, "You know grandma, I never thought Mimi would marry anyone but Jose." I wondered if Mimi's little indiscretion had been an affair of youthful passions or truly serious. I had been a little hurt by it and hoped that I could someday speak with Mimi to understand what her true feelings were for me.

Well, this chapter was meant to be devoted to Christmas, so I shall hurry on my way. Over the Thanksgiving holidays Jerry, Tim, Craig and Suzie helped Dad string up the Christmas lights. Mom

CHAPTER TWELVE   THE HO! HO! SEASON —AGAIN

wrapped the packages and I was very disappointed when Mom fitted them all into big boxes for Dad to take to the post office. They were on their way to the east coast for our family there.

Before Christmas, we made another trip to San Francisco and Mom made me to look as festive as the season. Again, cooler weather dictated that I wear my hair longer. And, guess what? This poodle-for-all-colors was white again! Don't question me too closely about my hair's vagaries. The French, I've been told, are a capricious lot. I certainly did not understand these changes, but the good Dr. Jackson assured Mother that these changes were normal. But he always assured Mom that I was a very special dog nonetheless. Oh yes, San Francisco....my hair always diverts me. As I said, I looked more magnificent than usual, for Mom had had a crochet hook in her hands for days, knotting brightly colored yarns. I remember wanting to play with the balls of yarn, but Mom said I would tangle them. She finally wrapped some yarn into a tight ball all for myself. that didn't last for long for I soon had my fill of yarn balls. I swallowed so much of the fibers I regurgitated. (Now how.... did I start with Christmas and end with my stomach reactions to yarn fiber? Patience, dear reader!)

Mom had made tunic dresses for all of her granddaughters, and my jealousy had been more visible than I thought for her hook had hooked a lovely red maxi-coat for me. It just cleared the floor and was scalloped all along the bottom. (Hold tight here con1es San Francisco!) The night she finished it, Mom and Dad walked me from the St. Francis Hotel to Magnins. The attention we attracted surprised even me. Some clods laughed, but there were many Ooh's and Ah's and admiring comments made up for the philistines.

However, there is no perfection in this universe, and certainly not in that lovely red coat. When I had to relieve myself, it was quite a tangle. I heard Mom tell Dad that she would have to shorten the length to a midi. I didn't care, for in those days, a midi was the very latest fashionable length.

Christmas came and went. We spent about ten days at home. We played on the golf course, rode on the cart, rode on bicycles. It was quite pleasant. My extensive travels had created an appreciation for home that most dogs will never know.

Mom was also pleased to be home. She managed to tuck in a few art lessons into her schedule. In the early spring, they had an amateur art festival in Palm Springs. So amateur that for five dollars anyone could show their paintings on Saturday and Sunday.

Mom joined a friend to share a stall at the festival. They stripped the walls of our home of paintings and took them to the exhibit hall. Mom also took me and my bed along. I couldn't quite understand what was going on-another human thing-but I was glad not to be left at home.

Our stall had more attention than any other- happy? or financially sad to say, it was not a matter of the paintings. The attraction--? Me!

Despite the attention, the day was boring. Mom wouldn't allow me to roam around, so I spent most of the day confined to my basket. I believe Mom found it a little boring too, because she never went back.

Chapter Thirteen
Mom's Interesting Ancestors

This chapter has no particular place in this history because it concerns Dad and his behavior when he has had a couple of drinks in the presence of company. Don't misinterpret me- Dad never got sauced, or stewed or inebriated, or any of the other myriad terms humans have for 'getting drunk.' He almost never had more than three drinks. I tell you this for I am about to tell you of Mom and her religion.

When we have company, religion almost always enters the conversation. Dad just has to tell a story which Mom confirmed as the gospel truth, even though she was always a little embarassed by it. Dad was just plain intrigued by it. One Saturday night, we had guests. The people were unimportant, but what I heard in their presence was. Religion was inevitably referred to. Dad turned on. "Do you realize that Bea is a famous person?" he asked, which was how he always led into the following story. The unanimous answer was no. So he filled them in while re-filling their glasses.

Dad's Story of Mom's Ancestors

Her grandfather, Edmond Ellsworth, was Brigham Young's (the number two man in the founding of the Mormon Church) only adopted son. He was adopted after marrying Young's eldest daughter, Elizabeth. She was not Mom's Grandmother, because her Grandfather-Edmond-was married to four women at the same time.

When the Mormons were persecuted for their religious beliefs, they decided to find a place where they could live their religion as "their conscience dictated." Brigham Young sent his scouts to find a place where the Mormons could migrate to.

Utah was not yet a state, which was most likely an important factor in its choice as a place to rebuild their homeland. Mormons wished to be out of the reach of Federal laws due to the fact that they were practicing polygamy. Human beings, unlike dogs, may only (lega1 1y) have one spouse at a time.

Mom's grandfather and other scouts decided on Salt Lake, in Utah, and returned to I11inois to inform President Young that a suitable place had been found. As the first group of Mormons entered the Salt Lake Valley, Brigham; who was very ill at the time was laying in the back of a wagon. He was helped to a sitting position so that he could view the valley below. He asked the question: "This is the place?"

Those very words are carved into a monument at that location, but the manner in which those words were spoken suffered alteration to become "This is the place." Many Mormons felt and feel that Young had a revelation about the place, rather than simply looking at a location advance scouts had selected.

Now I am not trying to re-write Mormon history according to my beliefs, contempt, affection, etc. Like a good (dog perspective) historian, I'm trying to be objective. The things I write are true, as I have seen Mom's grandfather's diary, in which this incident was recorded.

Shortly after the group settled in the

valley, Edmond Ellsworth took another wife, Mary Ann Dudley. But, in all fairness, he had to get permission from his first wife before he could take a second. I have seen pictures of the gentleman, and he was very handsome and tall, about six feet, two inches.

Sometime after settling in Utah, Mom's grandfather was sent on a mission to England. One can imagine the hardships of travelling in those days. I wish he had written more about his travels but he was such an active gentleman that he probably could not find the time. And, like we all do, he discounted the importance of day-to-day details that we find so terribly fascinating later.

Edmond was in England for two years. He converted many people to Mormonism, two of which were eighteen years old girls. One was Mary Ann Jones, who was Mom's grandmother, and the other was Mary Ann Bates. Edmond then received word that he was released from his English mission, as Brigham had appointed him the captain of the first handcart company of Mormons, who planned to cross the country to Utah on foot. This was a great honor to Edmond, and he hurried back to Nauvoo, Illinois. Among the people who requested to go the Utah on foot were the two Mary Ann's.

The ocean voyage would have been enough to discourage youngest women, but the Mary Ann's, who became good friends on the voyage, seemed to take strength from it. Now back in Nauvoo, Edmond, to his dismay, found that the hand carts were too flimsy to endure the hundreds of miles that lay between Illinois and Salt Lake.

All carts were about four feet by four feet and were going to be powered by human muscle. The few cattle accompanying them were to be driven, and the few horses were to be used to pull wagons with heavy supplies.

CHAPTER THIRTEEN   MOM'S INTERESTING ANCESTORS

After extensive alterations, Edmond finally gathered the people together, placed the two Mary Ann's at the head of the company, which numbered over three hundred people. His own belongings were stowed in the cart with the belongings of the Mary Ann's.

At this point of the story, I began to think Dad was a dirty old man-his imagination began tumbling like a rock polisher when he described the handsome Edmond heading this company of religious converts with two young, attractive girls at his side.

It seems that no matter how difficult the day's travel had been, the Mary Ann's could muster the energy to sing and dance after the meager meal had been prepared and eaten. Of course, Edmond was there, playing his clarinet, occasionally laying it aside to whirl the girls around the campfire. Dad always elaborated on the romancing he was sure went on between great-grandpa and the two Mary Ann's. There's no written record, but perhaps there was some hanky-panky (if I may use such an outmoded term). But, at the end of the three-month journey, Edmond had fallen in love with both girls, and they had fallen in love with him. Shortly after their arrival in the valley, great-grandpa secured the permission of his first two wives to marry the two Mary Ann's. Edmond, by the way, had come home to an enlarged family, for both wives had given birth to daughters in his lengthy absence.

At this point of the story, Dad's eyes lighted up with more of a leer than a gleam. The two Mary Ann's, it seems, were married to Edmond in the same ceremony. Brigham Young officiated and Edmond's first two wives attended, along with all the children.

Dad became over-dramatic at this point. He would pause, take a breath and say "you will never guess what happened." Our guests could never guess. A few months later, he told them, he had twins by his two young wives. If you assume that both wives had a set of twins you are wrong: each wife had a single child on the same day.

Mildly speaking, this implied that Edmond was quite a fellow, able to make two sweet young things happy and fertile at the same time. To tell you the truth, sometimes I wondered what all the excitement was about, but Dad always derived so much enjoyment from it. (And perhaps a bit of jealousy.) After the story had been told, Dad then told the guests that these early Mormons were 'supermen' for they neither smoked, nor drank coffee or liquor. Frankly, they couldn't help but be virile with the opposite sex. And, knowing human beings and their vices, being deprived of drinking and smoking, sex was the only pleasure left. Oh, the early Mormon men weren't a bunch of rip-snorting maniacs; they loved their women. But as I said before, love doesn't produce babies-sex does!

I heard several other anecdotes about this sexy-uh, virile gentleman. One that particularly amused me was also a bit of a comeuppance for Dad, who was a great joker. After enduring his jokes, Mom finally put one over on him. Mom and Dad had been on a trip to Arizona and on the way back to California, Mom suggested that they visit great-grandpa's 'estate.' They had only been married a short time, so when she suggested this little detour, Dad eagerly agreed.

At this time Dad knew very little about Mom's family, and so probably had visions of this great-grandpa being a wealthy man. No doubt, he probably thought, Mom would someday be an heiress. He gladly went a little out of his way to take a good look at this estate, which was outside of Yuma.

They took the highway to that desert city. As

Chapter Thirteen   Mom's Interesting Ancestors

they neared it, Dad questioned Mom as to the whereabouts of the estate. Mom kept saying she didn't remember the address, but that she would remember the route once they were near. They kept driving. Dad began to get a little perturbed when she continued to tell to keep driving. when they were all the way through Yuma, Mom suddenly said "make a fast right, and then a fast turn left." He did. And he found himself at the gates of the old Territorial Prison, otherwise known as the "Hell Hole." "This is the place?" he demanded.

Mom very coolly explained that it was indeed great-grandpa's estate. He had served a sentence there for polygamy.

Chapter Fourteen
Great Changes in Our Lives

A new chapter was written in our lives. It will take some concentration on my part to get the events in their proper order.

First of all, let me remind you that Mom and Dad had thirteen grandchildren, ranging from six to twenty-one years. That should give you a clue to the considerable amount of years my parents had already accumulated when I was first with them.

Most people reaching the so-called 'golden years' usually start to think about less work and more time in front of the television to doze. Not my parents. Their work and responsibility kept pace with their advancing years. And currently, everything they did involved me.

I was beginning, at this time in our history, to feel my years (around my fourth birthday). By human standards of age, I was a mature bachelor, and, unfortunately, had not had a single serious encounter. It was spring when I turned four and there were a lot of females in heat. I had gotten so full of love and affection again that Mom was having a hard time with me. I kept hoping that I could have some children soon.

Dad's firm believed in retiring their salesmen when reaching age 65. Dad became 65 the summer after the spring of my fourth birthday.

Neither Mom nor Dad liked the idea of enforced idleness, and when someone told Mom about a firm that might offer her a sales job, she applied. The job turned out to be more complicated that she anticipated, but sounded so interesting they decided to give it a try. And I stress 'they'. Mom and Dad never did anything by halves.

When Mom met the lady who owned the company, they liked each other so much that she asked Mom to take over the show room in the Los Angeles Merchandise Mart.

When I began to hear of all these new things. I was upset, feeling that I was witness to our happy home-life being sucked down the drain. But I soon understood that Mom would be at the showroom from five to nine Monday through Friday with Dad and me. Of course, the building rules stated that no pets were allowed on the premises. Honestly-if human beings love us so much, why were they always so busy denying us practically all right-of way? This rule was quite a blow, but I left it to these two dears to solve it.

They decided early on that had they been able to whip the airlines problem, they could whip our new office situation in much the same way. We would drive to the office, park, I would slip into the bag, and up we went to the eleventh floor where I had a basket under Dad's desk in a small private office. I slept a great deal of the time. Lethargy didn't exactly appeal to me, but I far preferred sleeping near them than romping around without them.

About one o'clock, Dad gave me a good walk and then concealed me again in the office. Now and then I was permitted to spend some time in the showroom, but only if the customer was a poodle lover. Fortunately, there were a lot of people who cared for us. God bless every one of them.

It was impossible to commute to Palm

Springs every day and hotels were very expensive. To save money, Mom and Dad found an apartment in the Los Angeles area.

We spent Monday through Thursday at the apartment, which was luxurious with two balconies, a fireplace, a swimming pool and a sauna.

On Friday, we happily returned to Palm Springs to spend the weekend. We were more stationary now, but we still did some travelling. We drove to San Francisco twice a month, then flew to Seattle and Portland. Once Dad flew to New York by himself.

Unsure of the success of the New York trip, it was decided that Mom should stay with the showroom while Dad did the traveling. The expense did not warrant all of us going.

To tell the truth, they would have saved money if both Mom and I had gone with Dad. You would not believe the phone calls. Those two dears could not bear to be separated. I went along with their feelings.

Chapter Fifteen
Troubles, Troubles

As you may have noticed in the last several chapter, I have only been reporting events of interest. After all, how much can you yak about walks, shampoos and airline chicanery without boring everybody to distraction? My life was delight to me but to subject a reader to a detailed schedule of delights, would not be so delightful.

At any rate, at this time of our lives, important events, and the troublesome and interesting-began rolling all over us, threatening at times to drown us. First, Mom's niece and her children stayed at our motel. They were on vacation and could not afford to do anything fancy, so they stayed at the motel rent-free for two weeks. Over one of the weekends, Mom's niece discovered a swollen gland under one of her children's arms.

Being a nurse, she immediately contacted her doctor. He thought it important enough to have the child checked out thoroughly at the U.C.L.A. Medical Center. We did not know until later that the doctor suspected leukemia. Dad drove mother and daughter to the center, where she underwent tests for the better part of the day. Thank goodness it did not prove to be a terrible disease. The young girl had problems, but correctable with medication.

After overcoming this scare, we found out that the lease at our office was up for renewal at the first on January. Dad was shocked when he learned the rent was being increased by two hundred dollars. Business had not been very good, and the room we had was much too large for our operation.

Dad located a smaller room on the third floor which would be a better location for us. Dad then had a partition placed at the back of the room so that I would have a private place for my bed and his desk. It was not as fancy as the old office but dressed up with pictures and paint, it sufficed.

I was pleased with the new location and soon had friends stopping in to say hello. However an enemy dropped in to say anything but a friendly hello.

One day, while Mom worked with a customer, a dumb, horrible clod came into our room and announced that he was the building manager. He had been informed that we had a pet in the room! He was very nasty; I shook in my bed. Dad ordered him out of the room and then followed him.

I was sure they would come to blows and half-de sired Dad to lay him flat. Fortunately, they cooled off before the affair became violent. Dad was told that if I were found again in the building, the lease would be terminated. After

Dad completely calmed down, he realized this was something of a boon to us, for we now knew how to break the lease. Sad to say, I was no longer able to be with my parents. I was left behind at the apartment. I was in no true pain, but I would still like to know who tattled on us. I would gladly tear his leg off and then maybe other portions of his anatomy. (Well, not really-but that violent statement shows you how angry I was.)

I now spent the mornings at the apartment. Dad arrived at about one o'clock to walk me and sometimes take me to the Mart to wait in the car until quitting time. The car, I hasten to add, was parked in a covered garage so I never suffered from thirst or heat. I never suffered from boredom either, for a garage is a surprisingly lively place. My days were anything but dull; matter of fact, it was more exciting than being in a nice, quiet office.

I was accident prone. One day, during this particular period in our lives, I heard Dad arriving for his mid-day visit. Naturally I gave him the royal welcome, or at least I tried to. I misjudged the simple jump to the floor from the couch and struck my front leg on the coffee table. I didn't want Dad to know of my clumsiness so I continued my greeting as if nothing had happened. But the truth will come out and the pain will too. By evening my leg was very lame. Of course, I still didn't let on, but one morning, when Mom picked me up for my daily brush, she discovered a large blood blister. Mom and Dad always became terribly shaken when they found anything wrong with me. They shook until the next day, Saturday, which meant that we would back in Palm Springs, and in the hands of Dr. Jackson, the only doctor Mom trusted with my lovely fur.

Fortunately, he did not consider my problem to be serious. He diagnosed the ugly blood blister for what it was-a severe bruise. He rubbed on

Chapter Fifteen Troubles, Troubles

some salve and wrapped my leg in a bandage. I felt much better. Mom felt better too after he gave her additional salve and instructions on care of the bruise. In a few days, my leg was well again, but I had lost all the hair around the bruise. Being terribly vain, I was not pleased with my appearance for several weeks, until the hair grew back.

Mom and Dad were not too happy with the new business, and so decided to look for a line or lines that would generate more interest. They tried a couple of lines that were not much better, and were becoming a little discouraged. Then, one day, a Chinese gentleman, a Mr. Yim Law, observed Mom sketching some dresses. He had a showroom in the Mart too, and was interested in Mom's work. He asked if she would design a line of dresses and pantsuits that he would manufacture in Hong Kong. If affairs turned out well, they would form a partnership. At first, Dad was skeptical, but soon realized he and Mom had nothing to lose but her time. A month later Mom had sketches ready for Yam's trip to Hong Kong.

Interestingly enough, Yam's main business was importing tropical fish, but he exported plastic and always had his eyes open for any item that might make money. Dad was wary of the fact that Yim was unsure of the venture's outcome, so he declined entering into a partnership. He and Mom were not young and did not want to invest money in the manufacturing end of the firm, preferring to sell the items on a commission basis.

For a while, all went well. Mom's designs looked good, and they sold well, but the finished stock had problems. Some of the fabric had spots, the sizes were not correct, and there were several other problems. Yim was sure that the problems could be corrected if Mom went to Hong Kong and conferred person ally with the manufacturers. Mom liked the idea, very much indeed. But Dad and I took a rather understandably dim view of the plan. We would be left behind to fend for ourselves-and we weren't good fenders! I could go on for pages about all the comforts and niceties we would be deprived of in her absences. I was sure that Dad would put his foot down (hopefully, stomp it down).

I was surprised and distressed when he agreed that it was the smart thing to do. I had understood that male of the human species was a stubborn, unreasonable lot, but he certainly proved that idea wrong. So again Mom made new sketches, took her shots, received her passport, and made all other necessary preparation for the journey.

She was only gone a week but it seemed like forever. I had never been away from her for a night. I was sure it was worse for Dad. I loved him dearly, but I worried over how he would brush, feed and love me, as well as taking care of other less important matters, like business. Apocalypse now!

I tried in every way to make her change her mind about going. I loved her with extra strength, I kissed more than ever. I clung to her like lint. When that failed to change her mind, I refused to eat, sulked, shifted my attention to Dad. Nothing worked. As time drew nearer and nearer for Mom to leave, Dad and I became unbearably sad. The night we took Mom to the airport, I finally reversed my policy of coldness and stayed in her arms. She held me until the last minute before she boarded.

I then cried until she was out of sight. I know I was being overly petulant, but I didn't care. We didn't want her happy when we were so forlorn. A very lovely Asian woman, who was on the same flight, patted my head before she boarded and told me to be a good boy. As it turned out, she and Mom became very good friends on the flight over.

Time clipped its wings that week. Things dragged. Dad did his best to make sure I looked nice, and was entertained. I didn't let him out of sight for a moment. I would have made a terrible orphan. I may sound as sophisticated as one of those legendary Astor poodles, but in truth, I was helpless without my Mom and Dad. Mom and Dad were seemingly helpless with out each other, for they phoned each other every night like the newlyweds they were not.

Dad and I were early to meet Mom's plane. Upon first sight of her, I squealed and struggled to leap out of Dad's arms and into hers. People around laughed at my behavior, but I didn't care. I was friendly, and I loved laughter. I was so glad to see her I couldn't stop licking her and crying. She looked tired and aged, but she was still beautiful, to me. I wouldn't let go until we climbed into the car. I then fastened onto her when placed on my pillow between them. I was so emotionally exhausted that I fell asleep so I didn't hear very much of their conversation about the trip. I did, however, gather that she enjoyed herself very much. She had dinner twice with ten Chinese gentlemen.

Dad was very silent when she told him this. I believe he was very jealous.

By the following day, all had fairly well settled down to normal. Mom and Yim felt the trip was worthwhile, but time would tell the true success. Sadly, success was nonexistent. The merchandise shipped from the Orient the next time was even worse that the first shipment. Mom and Dad told Yin they no longer wanted to have items manufactured outside of the United States.

For awhile, our new life in Los Angeles was up in the air.

Mom and Dad were perplexed as to our next step. They were not ready to give up and retreat in retirement to Palm Springs, but they were far from happy about their doubtful experiences in the wholesale ready-to-wear field.

Then, one day a friend of ours was in the showroom and Mom mentioned to her that she wished to find a good skirt line that would coordinate with a line of body suits that was currently selling well.

The friend asked Mom if she remembered a couple that had been in business in Palm Springs, operating under the name of 'Lamotte.'

Mom trusted the friend's word about the skirts and contacted Ted and Renee Lamotte to bring a sampling of their merchandise to the mart. They arrived the next day with the skirts, which excited both Mom and Dad.

To me, the skirts looked like scrambled messes, but Mom kept saying they were the most beautiful patchwork skirts she had ever seen, and sure to sell well at both wholesale and retail levels.

Mom and Dad tried for some instant reaction to the skirts. Mom placed a rather misleading sign in our window, which read 'sample sale.' This always snared the attention of the people working in the mart.

In a few days, we had taken orders for over fifty skirts. Women from all over the building snatched up the 12 skirts and wore them as they worked. It was the best possible method of advertising. No matter which floor or what type of merchandise the customers had come to buy at the Mart, they saw those skirts and inquired about them.

Frankly, I thought long skirts for daytime was a dumb fashion, but then again, I thought clothing itself was rather dumb. I occasionally wondered how and when human beings had lost their fur and had to resort to tubes and bags and other such things to cover themselves with. Dad also thought long skirts were a foolish idea. Being a man, he loved to look at pretty legs, and he didn't understand why a woman would wish to drag her hem on the floor. The dust the skirts dragged up made me sneeze. but our

Chapter Fifteen Troubles, Troubles

disappointment didn't matter when placed next to the good fortune of the Lamottes.

Within a few weeks, Ted and Renee were swamped with orders, and began working night and day. Soon, they had friends and relatives working night and day. Little did we know that when we and the Lamotte got together, the Lamottes were at the end of their financial rope. They had even accepted charity. We did discover that the Lamottes did not have enough available cash to pay for fabrics to produce the skirts that were in such sudden demand.

Dad, with his usual magnanimity opened a line of credit for them. Soon the Lamottes were able to move their work out of their garage and into a building large enough to set up their cutting tables and machines. We decided that our business also warranted a larger place for at times we were so busy we could not take care of our customers without making them wait.

With all the fuss, Mom and Dad sneaked me into the showroom, again. They just couldn't stand to leave me at the apartment. Frankly, can you blame them?

Chapter Sixteen
Terror

"This too shall pass," is an old saying. It means that all things pass, including the sunny times. Clouds gathered. It was a very hot August evening. We had just left the elevator for my last walk of the day. It must have been nine or nine-thirty, but with Daylight Savings Time, still dusky. There was a nice grassy spot at the entrance of the underground garage, and, at times, other pets and people joined us. But this evening, only Mom, Dad and I were there.

Suddenly there was a terrible screeching. A small sports car tore around the corner and careened into the garage entrance on two wheels. Dad and I avoided being struck by mere inches. The car then almost crashed into the garage wall. The driver managed to stop in time. He

Chapter Sixteen Terror

backed up, realigned his wheels and roared into the garage. We were so startled that Dad yelled, "What are you trying to do?"

We tried to calm down, and we continued to stand there, conversing as dog and masters do, over our close call. I was trying to work up some interest in the last stroll before bedtime, when, suddenly, the young man was coming toward us from the lobby of our building. When he was two feet from Dad he demanded "What did you say?" Dad looked at him. He then struck Dad on the cheek and nose. Dad reeled into the street, falling on his knees and elbows. He tried to get to his feet. The man then struck home on the mouth, knocking him back onto the sidewalk. By now, Mom was screaming and clawing at the man's back. She then ran into the alley next to the garage, trying to find something for a weapon. I think she would have killed him to save Dad. I was insane with fear for all of us and absolutely confused. I had never seen human beings acting like this.

Nobody came to help us. I know Mom could have been heard for blocks. Finally something distracted the man and Mom grabbed Dad by the shirt and pulled him away from the building. The man moved in the opposite direction. Mom continued to scream and tug on Dad. My leash was loose but I did not run. I was so frightened I couldn't even bark. Mom continued to scream for someone to call the police. It seemed to go on forever.

Finally, a man called down to us from an apartment. He told us he had phoned for the police and for Mom to bring Dad up. He met Mom at the bottom of the stairs and helped Dad. He was so bloody we couldn't tell where he had been hurt. Our helper took Dad to a basin and bathed his face with paper towels. I whimpered and lodged myself in corner. I had long ago learned that in such a situation I could best help by staying out of the way.

The police arrived about ten minutes later. They listened to half of the story and asked Mom if she could identify the car. She was sure she could. Taking me in her arms, she left Dad with good Samaritan and followed the police to the garage. We soon found the car, with its engine still hot. The police then asked Mom to return to Dad. With the help of our new friend, we managed to help Dad to our apartment. He was in terrible shape. Mom tried to clean him up a little more, but he was still in shock. Mom wanted to take him to emergency, but he just wanted to get into bed and get warm. In ninety degree heat, Mom turned the electric blanket all the way up to warm him.

After forty-five long minutes, there was a knock on the door. I was afraid for Mom to open it. A voice identified the knock as the police. Mom let them in. They looked at Dad and wanted to take him to the hospital. Dad wanted to remain in the bed. He had started to warm up, but he still shook. He promised he would see a doctor early the next morning. The police asked a a few more questions and peered into Dad's eyes with a flashlight. They then left us, and we had a feeling they knew where to find Dad's assailant.

We didn't sleep that night. The next morning, Mom located a doctor about a block away and managed to get dad into his office. He looked awful. I couldn't look at him without crying. We found out that his nose was broken and his elbow chipped. Bruises covered his face. His knees resembled pieces of raw meat and his arm was swollen to twice its normal size.

I was left at the apartment with Dad. Mom didn't want to leave, but she had appointments at the office that had to be kept. As miserable as Dad was, Dad left at noon to take a bus to

Chapter Sixteen Terror

the downtown office. I was so exhausted from the recent terrible events I slept on the bed until they returned at five thirty. While Mom prepared dinner, Dad stretched out on the bed. They both looked and felt awful. When they had fed me and were eating their own supper, they spoke of the terrible evening. All they could think of was to get out of that building. I advocated the plan. None of us would ever feel safe there again.

That very evening Dad talked to the building manager, who told Dad the police had been in touch with him. They knew exactly who the man was. He then told us that the building's owner had completed at another complex a few blocks away. Within three days we had moved into the new place. Sorry to say that in our haste to escape the old apartment building, we did not investigate the new property very well. The new place proved even less desirable than the former place. The buildings all around us were filled with loud, vulgar people who never seemed to go to bed. The only place we felt safe walking was in the garage, and what sort of place is that for walking? If you think that you would not blame us in light of recent events.

We soon looked for another place, and finally found one. This was a twenty-story building, complete with a pool and recreation area on the roof. We were about the same distance from work as we were in the old location. I loved the way we all looked for an apartment. Mom and Dad would make me as lovely as possible, take me in their arms, walk right up to the manager's apartment and asked if I were welcome. If I were not, they simply turned around and walked away.

A month later, after finding a place that welcomed me as I deserved to be, we were settled in a new apartment on the sixth floor, complete with balcony and plants. Here I could relieve myself, and so avoid a lengthy trek down six flights. I was finding as I got older I was more comfortable if I had a very convenient spot to use in the middle of the night.

This patio privy was also a blessing for Dad, for there were many times when he crawled out of a very comfortable bed when he realized I was in discomfort. Of course, I was discreet enough not to take unfair advantage of the situation and so used the patio only occasionally.

We were all very comfortable and private in our new apartment, and, on a clear day, through the southern window, we could almost see the ocean. After we moved in, Dad's unfortunate experience had a conclusion, but not a happy one. We were finally notified that the man had been found and was to be in court on a certain day to be identified and charged. This is a part none of us were proud of and I'm going to relate it quickly and not ask for your sympathy.

Dad had talked to the officer in charge of the precinct and Dad's brother who was an attorney. The officer told Dad frankly that his attacker would be out on the street after receiving a slap on the wrist, for his attack on Dad was his first offense. His brother, the attorney, was afraid we would endanger ourselves if we pressed the charges. We felt like cowards after we heard this. In short, we did not show up to pursue the case.

No, we did not feel right about our behavior. But Mom and Dad felt they were not young enough to perhaps get into a situation where they would be in danger from the family and/or friends of our assailant.

Mom told the officer that good people have to lock them selves in for safety, while the city is given over to the hoodlums. The officer agreed with her. It was frightening.

Dad once remarked that it was a 'dog-eat-dog world.' I began looking over my shoulder from then on when taking our evening stroll. I even became more alert when relieving myself. I always looked out of the corner of my eye, being sure that no one crept up on us. I have never suffered an injury that was not self-inflicted, but one never knows about the future. I was never quite sure after that terrible experience.

Chapter Seventeen
Trivia

The title indicates that this chapter is devoted to small incidents; but please don't think trivial. Importance is relative to the author and reader, so-oh, forget it! These are rather unin1portant incidents, but they are amusing, which gives them a kind of importance.

One night, while staying at the St. Francis, I required more water than usual, for I had had a spicy dinner. I had emptied my water dish by the time we went to bed. In the middle of the night I jumped down to get a drink and found that my dish had not been refilled. I whined my displeasure, but neither parent heard me. Soon. I was angry, as well as thirsty, so I picked up my little dish in my teeth, jumped back on the bed and plunked it on Mom's face. She let out a shriek which awakened Dad. They couldn't help but laugh when they realized my need and how my need had dictated my rather insistent actions. I had a similar tactic to show my disapproval of sloppy food-I flipped the dish over. Mom and Dad always laughed after they squawked.

One week Dad had overnight business in Los Angeles. Greg, a grandson, who was nine or ten at the time, made Mom decide to stay in Palm Springs, so he could enjoy the pool. Greg decided that it would be fun to sleep in the big bed with Mom because we had a great vibrator attachment. I loved it too, as a matter of fact.

Anyway this kid-pardon me, Greg-had a strange habit: he did not use a pillow. rather than putting it on a chair, he simply shoved it off the bed, which formed a ramp from the floor to the bed. Later that night, while dreaming, I felt the bed jerk. Mom suddenly jumped out of bed and snapped on the light. I was startled, not knowing if this were reality or an extension of my dream.

Then I saw a furry little creature leap off the bed. Mom and I then chased it to the bathroom. Mom turned on the light and shut the door. By now, Greg, the guilty one, was awake and staggering around, asking what all the commotion was about. Mom soon figured it out. A little field mouse had gotten into the house and used the pillow as access to the bed. It then scampered across Mom's face. I can imagine how that felt. Mom started to make sure that little mouse would feel something. She found a trap. I had never seen one before and I was glad I had not, for the little contraption looked lethal. My irritation with the mouse turned to pity when I saw her set it and place it in the bedroom, baited with a lovely bit of cheese. The little fellow had ticklish feet and bad timing; certainly not enough to require extermination at the courtesy of the sportsman like device.

We returned to bed. The next morning, we had the enemy dead in the trap. I couldn't look. Mom, the trapper, was shaken. She didn't even try to remove the little body from the trap; she threw the sprung device in the garbage pail. I don't blame her. It was pretty gruesome.

Chapter Eighteen
Mom Gives Us a Scare

Always remember those lovely lines of St. Paul and then couple it with the trite but true phrase "it never rains but it pours." If you can, life becomes acceptable, even if not particularly likable or understandable.

We were in San Francisco at the Palace Hotel. We had checked in the night before, Saturday. Sunday was the opening of a new show, which Mom and Dad were attending. Sunday morning, Mom said she did not feel well and didn't eat breakfast. By the time we opened the door of the front room to participate in the show, she looked gray. Her head and stomach hurt. Dad placed a large chair in the spacious bathroom and gave Mom a pillow. I stayed with her. I don't know if

Chapter Eighteen Mom Gives Us a Scare

my reaction was in sympathy, but I soon began vomiting too. Mom only wished she could do the same. Every little while, she would grow sick to her stomach, but could not get rid of it. As revolting as the act is, vomiting is healthy for the body, for it dispels food or liquid that the body cannot handle. She could only hold her stomach and groan. By the time we closed the door of the front room she was in poor shape. Dad took me for a walk and I felt better. I wish I could say so for Mom.

Finally, Dad became so worried that he called Mom's niece, the nurse who worked with a doctor. After describing the symptoms, the doctor told Dad to get Mom an E.K.G. Dad tried to find a doctor, could not, and Mom refused to go to emergency. Bluntly stated, we had a rough night.

The next day she was better, but her health was still poor. Dad got another room on the floor above the showroom and moved Mom there. Mom was able to get some rest. I stayed to keep her company. By that time, I was far from feeling well myself.

Dad dashed up every few hours to see how we progressed. By Tuesday she was better, but Dad refused to let her work. He looked tired, but he was healthy.

On Friday we drove home to Palm Springs. Mom's niece and Dr. Jack came that night; he insisted on listening to Mom's heart. He didn't like what he heard and called in a friend, who was also a doctor. They made an appointment for Mom to have a check-up immediately.

The next day, the new doctor listened to Mom's heart and then ran several tests. He then confirmed what Dr. Jack had surmised: she had had a heart attack. I didn't know what heart attack was exactly, but it sounded dreadful. Dad thought it was awful too.

Mom, however, took it well. The new doctor told Mom that under normal conditions he would have had her in the hospital in intensive care, but he felt that nothing would be accomplished by doing so. When I understood this, I was very glad that Mom would not be leaving us. Of course there many things were she was not supposed to do, and many types of medication she was supposed to take. I remember that she complained about the pills. She even hated to take aspirin.

She soon felt better, but began to lose weight, slowly. Her improved health was not accompanied by improved personality. In short, she was not her usual happy self. Once in a while, she had severe chest pains. After one especially bad attack, Dad called Palm Springs and talked to our doctor, who suggested a heart specialist in Los Angeles. We took his suggestion.

He placed Mom in the hospital for tests and possible open heart surgery. This time I was truly worried. I had no idea how long she would be gone. When I watched poor Dad, I began to think she would be leaving us forever.

Mom acted as though she were not afraid of what might happen. She tried to reassure Dad and me. We sweated out the three days they made her stay at the hospital. I don't exactly know what went on behind those walls, but I understood that they conducted several tests. One, called an angiogram, sounded awful. Dad told me that they opened up a vein in Mom's leg and ran a tube up through it to her heart. She was able to watch the procedure on a television. Mom's niece and Dr. Jack came to town to be there in case surgery was necessary.

I had previously refused to allow Artis, the nice niece to pick me up or fondle me, but I was feeling so forlorn that I welcomed her gladly. She was so surprised when I kissed her that she held me for a long time. By now, I not only needed comforting as a result of my fears over mom, but for creeping fears of this thing called death that

Chapter Eighteen Mom Gives Us a Scare

just might be stalking Mom. As a matter of fact, stalking all of us-sometimes this death attacked suddenly, for no reason, while letting others go. I hoped he would let Mom go.

All of the tests proved beneficial, and the doctors eventually decided against surgery and to give her liberty. But she could not tire herself and had to take nitroglycerine for medicine. I think that the simple act of quitting all the pills made Mom feel better. Dr. Jack told Dad something about a 'mitral valve' that was giving Mom trouble. To me, nothing was of great importance except for the fact that Mom was home again, nit roglycerine and all. Fear of death died.

But Mom still failed to improve. And a few months later, death stalked about our household when she was rushed into an emergency operation. And finally the truth was out: She had a tumor, which required a hysterectomy to remove. I heard Mom protest that she was too old for that type of problem. But this terrible time soon proved to have benefits, as she could not work for four to five weeks. She stayed in Palm Springs with me. I loved it.

Dad would go into Los Angeles for three days a week and then we were all together for the four other days. Gradually Mom's problems were overcome. She gained weight, her heart improved and we were all very happy once more.

Mom began to find it a little difficult to keep me looking beautiful. She kept up the usual schedule of bathing me once a week, brushings twice daily and a trim and pedicure every three to four weeks. But my fur wasn't cooperating. It was thinning on my back legs.

If Mom wasn't careful in the brushings, freckles were visible. She let the hair grow a little longer and then brushed it back and forth until I looked up to standard. I hoped that I hadn't caught

Dad's lack of hirsuteness. He looked like Telly Savalas or Yul Brynner-that is, handsome, but very bald. Mom said he was better looking than ever with a shiny pate, which tells you how much she loved him.

She also joked that all those silly cults which shaved their heads are filled with men all going bald.

I couldn't turn my head far enough to observe my thin spots, but I do know I wasn't in danger of going bald. But I was losing enough hair to concern the folks. When Mom took me for my booster shots, she asked Dr. Jackson about my problems. He gave Mom some vitamin pills big enough for a horse that I ignored because I wasn't a horse. I grew furious when he told Mom that my thinning hair was due to advancing age.

Then melancholy set in. I knew that I was no longer a puppy. Several birthdays slipped by, almost unnoticed, because my life had been too interesting to notice. I claimed it was a case of 'who counts?' but Dr. Jackson had been counting. I began to face up to some raw facts. In that last year I had not been as interested in female poodles as I once had been. I was yet searching for the right one, but Jackson's words made me realize I was still searching. But, I told myself, celibacy was not the worst form of life, and did I really have the patience for puppies?

Time was passing me by. No-I didn't feel a bit older. I did like to take longer naps. But I had started that several years before. I had found being in the showroom boring, and lengthy naps helped to pass the time. I finally had to admit that I was rationalizing. I was growing older.

One day Mom started a painting. She drenched the canvas with lovely colors and had Dad hold me in his arms. She would look at me and then dab at the canvas. Imagine my

Chapter Eighteen Mom Gives Us a Scare

delight and surprise when she finally let me see what she had painted a likeness of me.

I was perched on a big blue cushion, my head slightly tilted, and completely surrounded by pastel clouds. I forgot my age in vanity, wondering how many other pets had had their portraits done in oil. I was even more delighted when she framed and hung it in the showroom above her desk. Anyone entering could not avoid looking directly into it. Mom received many compliments and several commissions to paint pets. I was the only one she did from life; all others she worked up from pictures. The pay was excellent; however, she did not want to work commercially. She liked to paint what she liked to paint and an agent would make her paint by assignment. Humph! You can't demand art! It must be a reflection of an image within the soul. Even poodles know that!

Before the painting was hung, I was rather famous, but after it went upon the wall, many people would actually inquire after me. Sometimes they would call me 'Pedro' or 'Juan' or some other Spanish name, but I was not terribly offended by their errors. At least, they remembered to ask about me, and had the cultural ballpark of my name.

For a while, I thought my travelling experiences were to be broadened. Mom and Dad began speaking of a trip to the Far East. In fact, Dad took some of the shots that were required to renew his passport. Just as I began to wonder if I would also need shots (and detesting the idea) I heard my folks talking about an old friend and neighbor who would be "very good to me, 'and how' she truly loved me.' They were planning on leaving me behind.

I tumbled into a fit of depression. I was so down that I actually desired to take shots so that I could go. Of course, they only wanted the best for me, and leaving me home would have been the best. I know I was being selfish, but all I could think at the time was how unnecessary the trip sounded. Some of the things they planned on doing and seeing sounded dumb. Even the food they looked forward to eating sounded strange.

For three weeks I listened to them talk about the places they wanted to see, the foods they wanted to eat, the planes to catch, so on and so forth. I was worried to death, I wondered, what if some thing happened to them? I loved Bobby, the neighbor, but to live out the rest of my life without Mom and Dad was unthinkable.

I struck a hard, stony bottom of despair. My appetite fled. The folks soon worried over my loss of weight. They decided not to go. I don't know if their decision was made because of business reasons, for the trip was to be a combination of business and pleasure, or because they didn't want to leave me when I was sick.

No matter what the reason, the trip was cancelled. I was so relieved I could barely contain myself, and began to relish food again. My depression gave way to the joy of living and I soon forgot my fears over death.

Chapter Nineteen
Pleasure and Sorrow

We had planned several times to take a trip to Solvang, a small, mostly Danish village, about thirty miles north of Santa Barbara. One of Dad's favorite business contacts wanted to go there too, so we decided to finally make the trip in one group. I was looking forward to this trip, for the people were pet lovers too, and had a little friend about my age and size.

Mom had used me for a model for a coat she had made for their pet as a Christmas gift. I really don't know why, but I assumed that their pet was a female. The trip became more than anticipated, it became titillating.

And then, the evening before we left, I had an accident. My usual agility was belied by weakness in my hind legs. When I jumped from the bed to the floor, I twisted my left hip. It hurt like the lowest circle of hell. Mom went to pieces as she always did when I injured myself. She rubbed my hip and straightened the leg out, but it was still painful to stand on it. If I held it a certain way I was all right, except when it came to walking- or should I say hopping, on three legs. My walks were cut short. When I grew tired, Mom or Dad would pick me up and carry me.

Our friends arrived at noon the next day. I was very disappointed that I could not even be friends with their Standard Poodle, for he was exceedingly ill tempered. I took no joy in the trip. Sometimes, when he got into a strange mood-that is, nice and playful-his romping was too rough and my lame leg suffered. I let Mom know I would rather be myself than in the same room with him.

Of course, she understood my desire. She also knew I was not feeling very well, for a virus had decided to keep company with my bad leg. I was eager to sleep and eat only.

Even though I performed the role of a wet blanket to perfection, Mom and Dad still enjoyed their trip very much. Solvang is nestled in a valley formed by rolling hills, and was once visited by the King and Queen of Denmark. Solvang is noted for its delicious bakery goods and Mom and Dad sampled everything. Bread and cookies were not my favorite foods, but I enjoyed the tidbits they fetched for me. The rest of the food was excellent as well. One night I had some pot roast, another night a tiny bit of filet.

I had heard them speak of an open air theatre, which was recommended as one of the things to do in Solvang. I was rather glad when they left me to enjoy whatever went on in an open air theatre, for I wanted to relax and sleep. If I had been included, I would have had to share a seat with Mom and that would have been tortuous to my lame leg.

I found out when they came back that they had seen a play, and they had enjoyed it. They were not too late returning, and loved me up nicely before taking me out to relieve myself one last time before retiring.

On our way back to Los Angeles, we took a different route which wound through the mountains and lakes. They would often stop so that I could stretch my legs. Each time they watched me carefully to see if I might use my bad leg.

I'm afraid I disappointed them; I could not bear to stand on it. But the trip home was still very pleasant. I always enjoyed picnics. We stopped at a lake of Edenic loveliness, which was being used by happy people. Mom and Dad were happy too when the attending ranger said that I was welcomed. I remember hoping that we would return there someday, to that lovely paradise. But fate had other plans-plans that were strangely familiar?

Chapter Twenty
Pet Heaven

I began to believe in bad and good luck. I would go months without hurting myself, and then I could not do anything without spraining a leg or injuring myself in some fashion.

There came a time when the stars all seemed to operate against us. As soon as we arrived home from our Solvang trip, Mom made an appointment with Dr. Jackson to check my leg. I was more than willing to go as I was becoming tired of the ache.

As usual, Dr. Jackson was very gentle. He carefully worked my hip joint back and forth, and then there was a funny little click. My leg was fine, if tender. The good doctor had done it again. I limped, but could at least put my paw down.

The doctor gave Mom some pills to help the strained muscles, which relieved me, for I was afraid I might be in for more surgery. My reprieve was short-lived.

That very evening, I jumped off the chaise lounge and sprained the other hind leg. Fortunately, the leg I had sprained was now strong enough to support me, even though it pained me to use it. Next day, we headed back to the doctor. He was very sympathetic and gentle, and worked for a long time to make me comfortable. When I left for home I was not in pain, but I had been given a painkiller. There were more pills to take and I was to be kept quiet. The next few days were foggy. The medication kept me comfortable, but also put my wits on hold.

Gradually, I started to mend and by the next weekend was able to limp around, using all four legs. But I did not feel as lively as usual. All the pills, shots and medication were taking their toll. I heard somehow that each accident, illness, or operation, took away so many months and years from your life expectancy. If this were true, I realized this little accident-prone poodle was in trouble.

My health problems would not allow me to jump up on the bed, or even chairs. Little dogs do a great deal of this. We like to view things from a higher perspective. Mom and Dad understood and were always watching me. When they saw me contemplating a jump to anything over a foot high they immediately picked. me up and placed me on it. They were right and tender in doing so. They wanted me to avoid any more strain to my lame back legs. I was more or less grounded. I no longer slept on the bed. Mom placed me on the bed and gave me a little romp, but not the boisterous free-for-all we had once enjoyed.

I kept hoping that my rear end would strengthen, but it did not. I finally reconciled myself to the grim fact that my frisky days were over. I began to sleep more and more in the daytime, and it was not affecting my ability to sleep at night.

I knew that the folks were concerned about me and to tell the truth I was worried about myself. My health continued to deteriorate. Little things no doubt. Symptoms of failing organs, starting to manifest themselves. For instance, on evening after a normal dinner I just couldn't get enough water. Mom filled my dish four times and each time I erupted it without stopping. Then I upchucked and begged for more water. Again I up chucked.

Finally in desperation Mom picked up my dish and would not let me have any more. I was still very thirsty, but realized that I couldn't go on with that routine. Thank goodness the next day was Friday and we would be in Palm Springs. Mom called for an appointment with the Doctor. This was one time I approved. The Doctor really looked me over.

He finally told: Mom that he was concerned with the results of the examination and that he wanted to do some tests. He wanted Mom to leave me do some of the tests could not be run right then. He said they could pick me up in the late afternoon. I hated to stay, but did not feel well enough to put up a fight. As soon as Mom left they started the tests.

The tests consisted of taking blood samples, (which I hate,) those needles scare the devil out of me, besides they hurt. The tests also included taking urine samples and x rays. Then they inserted a large needle under the skin on the back of my neck and let a water solution drip into my dehydrated body. I did not like the procedure, but had to admit that afterwards I was more comfortable. The awful thirst subsided and I was

Chapter Twenty Pet Heaven

quite comfortable. By the time Mom came to pick me up I had enjoyed a nice nap, but I was very glad to see her. The Doctor had Mom go into his office to explain what they had found from all of the tests. I had been given some sort of sedative so was not too alert. but even in my stupor I could tell that the doctor was increasingly concerned with me. Mom's voice was low and strained when she asked him what 'renal failure' meant. Dr. Jackson gravely explained that my kidneys were failing. If the process were not reversed, I would die.

All of this sort of floated over my head. I was not terribly concerned with his words or manner, for I was comfortable in Mom's arms. I was glad when she took me home. But I felt Death stalking me. But Death was not frightening, at least, not like that terrible black man in Los Angeles. But still, Death was not for me. I knew I was sick, but I assumed that the good doctor would take care of me as he had always done and I would soon be well.

Each day Mom would take me to the hospital. They injected fluid under my skin to keep me from dehydrating. Dr. Jackson told Mom that he hoped my condition would improve and that my kidneys would start to function again on their own. Each day Mom returned to pick me up. I would try to show her how much appreciated that she did not leave me there overnight. I didn't know if I convinced her. I was no longer me.

I looked terrible. That was a bad blow to this vain poodle. After each treatment I had a huge bag hanging under my chin. My body gradually absorbed the moisture over a period of several hours. For my comfort, Mom and Dad made a large bed out of outdoor furniture mats on the living room floor. This was not only for me, but for them as well. I slept in the center while they flanked me.

I was so weak I could barely move. At times I would vomit. When I was not in the hospital, Mom would drop water and baby food into my mouth with an eyedropper. I couldn't even stand up to eat. Each day it was becoming more difficult to swallow. Mom placed a large pillow on a serving cart and placed me on it. She would roll the cart to wherever she had to be so that I would be with her and high enough to watch. I hardly cared. I had once been so intrigued in anything that interested them. I was turning inwards, making acquaintance with the stalker.

After the third day of my decline, I finally admitted to the presence of Death. I was not too sad or in pain. As I had realized before, Death, although mysterious, was not frightening. But it did sadden me to see Mom and Dad looking so heartbroken. They were losing weight and getting very little sleep as they tended to me. Sometimes tears rolled down Mom's face. I wanted to comfort her, to tell her that I was on the right road, but I was too weak except to kiss her hand and show my love for her in my eyes. I knew she would see and understand.

She still bathed and brushed me, for she knew that I did not want to become ratty and ugly, even if my only guest was Death, who patiently waited for me. They did not go into Los Angeles to work; they spent every minute caring for me. After eight more days I was almost anxious for the moment when I could depart with my new friend Death into the life in which I could never be ill or in pain.

Dr. Jackson told Mom and Dad that nothing could be done to save my life. He suggested euthanasia. Mom could not consent. I vaguely understood what they spoke about and did not care. I realized that Mom won out. When Dr. Jackson assured her that I was not in pain, she decided to keep me with them as long as I could recognize them and their love for me.

Chapter Twenty Pet Heaven

On the tenth day, I could not even raise my head. The doctor told Mom there was no longer any reason to continue treatments. They could only do "what was necessary" to keep me comfortable. They took me home and cared for me. To the end, they never left me in the hospital longer than they had to.

I was glad to be at home. Soon I was not sure if I were hallucinating or seeing things as they truly were. Perhaps I was being allowed to see things the well and living cannot.

There was a beautiful place in the distance, a mixture of all the fairways, woodland lakes, lovely hotel rooms that I had seen in my life. I thought I saw my poodle mother waiting for me. She had drowned in the pool at her home in Fresno six months before. I had been sorry that I had not been able to visit her again before her death... but now she was visiting me. Why, she was Death! As she had once awaited my birth, bore me and cared for me, she now stood ready to perform the compassion offices during my death.

She had once told me "I will be there at the end." So she was. The place in back of her became all rolling hills and skies of lovely pastel colors, just like the background of my portrait. Once, when someone asked Mom where she had gotten the idea for the soft colors surrounding me, she said "Oh! That is poodle heaven."

It was October ninth. I would not have been ten years old until February eighth, but I once heard Dad say "It was not the length of life, but he quality of life that was important." I had lived a beautiful life. If I could have regained my health, I would have gladly stayed with my folks, but my Death was an escape from a life that was becoming increasingly unbearable.

Two nights earlier Mom had moved back to the king-sized bed. She knew that I could not move myself so she placed the cart next to the bed and kept her hand on me all night. This last night she and dad took turns walking with me in their arms. At about three in the morning she placed me between them on the bed. I loved that time in the last hours, but I was unable to let them know. I was quite aware that I was soon to die. I am sure Mom and Dad knew too.

The sun rose. At eight o'clock, my poodle mother became real in a cloud of rainbow colors. I took my last breath of diseased life and suddenly I became real in the cloud 'too. Life became death, but then death became life, a new and eternal one. I greeted my poodle mother and wept for my Mom and Dad. I wished- and wish Now-I could let them know how glad I was to have escaped from that sick little shell, whose white curls looked lovely, but also vaguely silly. If I could, I would tell them that I will be with them at the last as well, as my poodle mother promised me.

Then Mother and I began the journey to the pastel hills.

The End

www.ingramcontent.com/pod-product-compliance
Lightning Source LLC
Chambersburg PA
CBHW071704040426
42446CB00011B/1902